chronicle
99

Dorling Kindersley
LONDON, NEW YORK, DELHI, SYDNEY

Publisher Mike Edwards
Co-ordinating editor Ian Paton
Editor Nicki Lampon
Design manager Louise Dick
Production manager Sara Gordon

Produced for Dorling Kindersley by
GRANT LAING PARTNERSHIP
48 BROCKWELL PARK GARDENS
LONDON SE24 9BJ

Project editor Lee Stacy
Design director Ruth Shane
Editorial director Reg Grant

Written by Reg Grant

Picture researchers Will Hoon and Jo Walton
Indexer Kay Ollerenshaw

PUBLISHER'S NOTE
Chronicle 99 covers events of the period mid-November 1998 to mid-November 1999 – a full 12 months of news. It takes up where *Chronicle 98* leaves off and will be followed, in the same manner, by the 2000 edition, which will include a full record of the millennium celebrations and news events. The 2000 edition will be published in December 2000. Meanwhile, readers can view a regularly updated record of news events for the whole millennium period by looking at the Dorling Kindersley web site address **www.dk.com/daybyday**

First published in Great Britain in 1999
by Dorling Kindersley Limited
9 Henrietta Street, London WC2E 8PS

A CIP catalogue record for this book is available from the British Library
ISBN 0 7513 0823 4

Reproduced by Goodfellow & Egan, Peterborough
Printed in Spain by Printer Barcelona

For our complete
catalogue visit
www.dk.com

chronicle 99

A year of news as it happened

Mid-November 1998 to mid-November 1999

A Dorling Kindersley Book

End of millennium highs and lows

During the last year of this millennium, there was plenty of evidence to support the views of those prophets of doom who believe the world is heading for an apocalypse. There were wars, earthquakes and other natural disasters, tragic accidents, and bombings and murders aplenty. Yet, as ever, there were also signs of the ability of the human spirit to rise above adversity. Even in war-torn Kosovo, the perpetrators of crimes against humanity were sent packing and the Kosovan people were able to regain their homes.

A well-placed spectator celebrates as the Queen passes on her way to open the first Scottish parliament for almost 300 years.

Among the events that stood out in the year was the unexplained murder of TV presenter Jill Dando, a person who epitomized ordinary good nature and cheerfulness. People were also shocked by a series of bombings in London apparently aimed at gays and ethnic minorities.

But this dark news was offset by the general buoyancy of British life, entering the new millennium with a stronger economy and more optimistic attitudes than for many years. The British spirit was visible in the performance of the footballers of Manchester United, who won the European Cup with a memorable

TV presenter Jill Dando, inexplicably shot dead on her doorstep.

"A lively, loving, beautiful light was extinguished."

Reverend Roger Collins, speaking at Jill Dando's funeral

demonstration of fighting spirit to the last minute. It was also summed up in the modest hero Brian Jones, the British half of a pair of balloonists who at last managed the feat of flying nonstop around the world.

Britain's constitutional landscape was changing, as the hereditary peers prepared to bow out of the House of Lords, and the Scots and Welsh elected their own parliament and assembly. This wave of modernization was sure to give Britain a new look in the new century.

The millennium drew to a close with modest hopes for a better world, but no great expectations.

Gary Neville, David Beckham, and Jaap Stam celebrate Manchester United's win over Bayern Munich in the European Cup final.

Environmental activists attacked fields of genetically modified crops, donning white protective clothing to dramatize their cause.

The Paddington rail crash in October killed 30 people and propelled the issue of rail safety to the top of the public agenda.

"This is not a battle for territory, it is a battle for humanity."

Prime Minister Tony Blair on the war in Kosovo.

Kosovan refugees were driven from their country in tears (left), but returned in joy showing their gratitude to Nato liberators (below).

The race to complete the first nonstop round-the-world balloon flight was won at last, by Betrand Piccard and Brian Jones.

It was a year of major earthquakes: here, a hotel in Taiwan has been knocked on its side by a huge tremor.

…Britain and other imperial powers joined forces to crush the Boxer uprising in China, a revolt against foreign domination…

…Boer farmers in South Africa took up arms against the British, beginning a long and brutal colonial war…

…a bewhiskered Conservative, Lord Salisbury, was prime minister…

…and spectacular buildings were erected in Paris for a World Exhibition that celebrated the arrival of a new century.

Two World Cups and sporting hiccups

There were high sporting achievements to celebrate in 1999, but unfortunately for British fans, most of the best performances were by foreign teams and stars. With the glittering exception of Manchester United football club, victorious at home and in Europe, Britain's sports personalities made more headlines for near-misses than for successes. Britain hosted two World Cups in the course of the year, in cricket and rugby. Both competitions provided colourful spectacle and some superb matches, but neither England's cricketers nor the British rugby teams capitalized on home advantage.

Pakistan fans give their team enthusiastic support in the cricket World Cup.

Kevin Keegan took the place of Glenn Hoddle as England football coach without solving the national side's problems. Ultimately, England and Scotland found themselves in a straight fight to qualify for Euro 2000. In tennis, Tim Henman held his place as one of the world's top players and reached his second Wimbledon semi-final, only to lose again to Pete Sampras. Formula One driver Eddie Irvine surprised everyone by making a serious challenge for the world championship, but ended as runner-up. And in golf's Ryder Cup, Europe, amid controversial scenes of American rejoicing, lost to the US after seeming to have victory in their grasp.

The rugby World Cup brought a spectacular victory for France over New Zealand (above). The enthusiasm of British fans (below) failed to inspire the home teams to success.

"When we needed to stand up and be counted, we weren't up to it."

England cricket coach David Lloyd, on the team's early exit from the World Cup

Pedro Diniz somersaults out of the European Grand Prix during a Formula One season rich in thrills and spills.

Lennox Lewis needed two tries to take the world crown from Evander Holyfield.

Paul Scholes scores one of his three goals against Poland, a rare success for the English national team.

…motor racing had just taken off as a sport…

…footballers wore plenty to keep warm…

"The most disgusting scenes I have ever seen on a golf course."

European vice-captain Sam Torrance on American golfers celebrating their Ryder Cup win.

Tim Henman was again the "almost" man, reaching the Wimbledon semifinals.

Americans display their joy at winning the Ryder Cup.

…cricket was an upright, dignified sport…

Dean Macey emerged as a rising star in British athletics, winning a silver medal for the pentathlon in the World Championships.

…and teams at the 1900 Olympics were genuine amateurs with limited training.

Love and marriage, money and divorce

British fashion designer John Galliano outraged the animal rights movement with a display of luxurious outfits rich in fox fur.

Marriage was very much in the air in the last year of the millennium. Prince Edward at last followed his brothers out of bachelorhood. He hoped that a more private and low-key approach to getting wed would help reverse the Royal Family's disastrous recent record of marital failure. Low-key is hardly a term that could be used to describe the wedding of footballer David Beckham and Posh Spice Victoria Adams, married in regal splendour in an Irish castle four months after the birth of their child, Brooklyn. Zoe Ball and DJ Fatboy Slim opted for discretion and gave the press the slip at their very different media wedding.

But divorce, and the mind-boggling sums of money it could cost, were equally a theme of the year. Hollywood rumours suggested that actor Michael Douglas intended to agree to a £40 million divorce settlement so he could be engaged to fashionable Welsh actress Catherine Zeta-Jones. Media mogul Rupert Murdoch went through a high-cost divorce and married 32-year-old Wendy Deng. But Mick Jagger and Jerry Hall did not divorce, as a judge ruled they had never been married.

The huge sums of money changing hands in divorces was typical of a year in which *Do You Want to Be a Millionaire?* was the hit TV show and the biggest movie, the *Star Wars* prequel *The Phantom Menace*, was rated not on its dubious artistic merits but on its huge box-office takings.

"We're the best of friends who also happen to love each other."

Prince Edward, Earl of Wessex

The Queen's youngest son, Prince Edward, married Sophie Rhys-Jones in informal style, a private rather than a state occasion.

Actor Michael Douglas (above) was enjoying life at the age of 55 with his new love, Welsh actress Catherine Zeta-Jones.

Darth Maul, face of the year from the Star Wars *prequel* The Phantom Menace.

Actress Gwyneth Paltrow won one of Shakespeare in Love *'s seven Academy Awards.*

Chris Tarrant, quizmaster in the hit ITV show Do You Want to Be a Millionaire?

"He's really deep, which I like."

Victoria Adams on her husband, David Beckham

Footballer David Beckham and Posh Spice Victoria Adams had a baby, and married in a fairytale-like Irish castle.

Radio presenter Zoe Ball married DJ and musician Fatboy Slim.

On a somewhat uncomfortable visit to Argentina, Prince Charles tangoed with dancer Adriana Vasile.

When the century began...

...Lillie Langtry was a prominent actress and the mistress of the Prince of Wales...

...Dr Sigmund Freud was working on revolutionary ideas about sex and dreams...

...and Queen Victoria was on the throne, flanked here by her eldest son, Edward, the Prince of Wales (left), and his son, George.

No longer with us

Raisa Gorbachev, wife of former Soviet leader Mikhail Gorbachev, died aged 67.

Director Stanley Kubrick led a reclusive life. He made only 12 movies in his career.

Iris Murdoch's career as a novelist and philosopher was cut short by Alzheimer's.

Sir Dirk Bogarde won acclaim for his roles in movies such as The Servant *and* Darling.

Cardinal Basil Hume, the Archbishop of Westminster, lost his fight against cancer.

Screaming Lord Sutch brought a zany humour to the business of electioneering.

Frankie Vaughan, whose theme song was "Give Me the Moonlight", died aged 71.

Dusty Springfield, one of the leading female vocalists of the 1960s, made a comeback in the 1980s singing with the Pet Shop Boys. Her deep, sensual voice was much admired.

Oliver Reed was almost as well known for his drunken misbehaviour as for his acting.

Chronicle 99

A year of news as it happened
Mid-November 1998 to mid-November 1999

How Chronicle 99 works

Chronicle 99 presents the major events from mid-November 1998 to mid-November 1999 as reported in the media at the time that they actually happened. It allows you to follow the progress of the most important events as they unfolded over the year.

The period covered over two pages is detailed here

This indicates which month you are in

The yellow tint shows which days are covered

Forward links appear like this (→ May 31). They direct you to a continuation of the story

Brief details of various news and sporting events are listed here

Articles present main news events as they were reported on the day

Brief obituaries are found here

November

S	M	T	W	T	F	S
1	2	3	4	5	6	7
8	9	10	11	12	13	14
15	16	17	18	19	20	21
22	23	24	25	26	27	28
29	30					

Baghdad, 15
Iraqi dictator Saddam Hussein agrees to allow UN inspectors unconditional access to suspected illegal weapons sites, averting the threat of joint American and British airstrikes. (• December 17)

Westminster, 16
The use of laboratory animals to test the safety of cosmetics ends as companies accept a voluntary ban under pressure from the government.

London, 17
Footballer Geoff Hurst, who scored a hat trick in the World Cup final of 1966, is knighted by the Queen.

Westminster, 18
Paymaster General Geoffrey Robinson is forced to apologize to the House of Commons for a series of breaches of the House's rules on disclosure of outside financial interests. (• December 23)

New York, 20
Vincent Van Gogh's *Portrait of the Artist without Beard* is sold for $71.5 million (£44 million) at Christie's, becoming the third most expensive painting ever.

London, 25
The Law Lords rule by a 3–2 majority that extradition proceedings can go ahead against former Chilean dictator Augusto Pinochet. Spain wants to try General Pinochet on charges of murder, torture, and genocide. (• December 9)

London, 25
Jane Couch becomes the first woman to contest a professional boxing match in Britain, defeating Simone Luke in the first round. Last year, Couch won a sexual discrimination case against the British Boxing Board of Control, which had denied her a professional licence.

Dublin, 26
Tony Blair becomes the first British prime minister to address the Irish parliament. He calls on them to "forgive and forget age-old enmities".

DEATHS
November 15. Kwame Ture, formerly known as Stokely Carmichael, Trinidad-born leader of the 1960s Black Power movement in the United States, dies in Guinea, West Africa, aged 57.

November 29. Robin Ray, broadcaster, entertainer, and popularizer of classical music, dies aged 65.

12

BRUSSELS, MONDAY 23

EU votes to lift beef export ban

European Union farm ministers voted this evening to lift the ban on the export of British beef imposed 32 months ago at the height of the scare over BSE, or "mad cow disease". Only the German minister voted against ending the ban.

Speaking for hard-pressed British farmers, Ben Gill of the National Farmers' Union said: "It is the best Christmas present we could have." The decision will not take effect immediately, however. Britain has first to complete a cull of potentially infected cattle, and EU inspectors will need to satisfy stringent new conditions. The actual resumption of exports is expected to take place next spring.

The BSE crisis led to the slaughter of four million cattle and has cost taxpayers some £4 billion. The government acknowledges that it will be a long time before confidence in British beef is restored. (• March 1)

KAZAKHSTAN, FRIDAY 20

Space station project takes off

The core module of the International Space Station in orbit around the Earth.

The biggest space project since the manned flights to the Moon got under way today when a Russian Proton rocket blasted off from Baikonur in Kazakhstan, carrying the first section of the International Space Station (ISS) into Earth orbit.

The ISS is a joint project by the United States, Russia, Japan, Canada, and nine European states, including Britain. It will take six years to complete, involving almost 100 rocket launches and 160 space walks.

The eventual cost of the ISS has been variously estimated at between £10 billion and £60 billion. The United States is expected to foot most of the bill. (• May 31)

New York, Monday 16. Senator John Glenn and his wife, Annie, were treated to a ticker-tape parade through Manhattan today, celebrating the US senator's feat in crewing a space shuttle mission at the age of 77. The nine-day mission, aboard *Discovery*, has revived enthusiasm for the US space programme.

November 15–30, 1998

...ition of Lords

...ion whose traditional ritual may soon face radical reform.

...rd for ...ng vast ...peters.

PARIS, WEDNESDAY 18

Victory for MI5 renegade Shayler

A French court today delivered a stinging rebuff to the British government by ruling that former MI5 officer David Shayler should not be extradited to face charges under the Official Secrets Act. Shayler had broken Britain's strict secrecy laws by leaking to the press embarrassing details of alleged MI5 incompetence and malpractice.

Accepting Shayler's argument that he was a victim of a political prosecution, the French court ordered his immediate release. At the prison gates, Shayler told the press that it was "a great day for justice".

13

S	M	T	W	T	F	S
1	2	3	4	5	6	7
8	9	10	11	12	13	14
15	16	17	18	19	20	21
22	23	24	25	26	27	28
29	30					

Baghdad, 15
Iraqi dictator Saddam Hussein agrees to allow UN inspectors unconditional access to suspected illegal weapons sites, averting the threat of joint American and British airstrikes. (→ December 17)

Westminster, 16
The use of laboratory animals to test the safety of cosmetics ends as companies accept a voluntary ban under pressure from the government.

London, 17
Footballer Geoff Hurst, who scored a hat trick in the World Cup final of 1966, is knighted by the Queen.

Westminster, 18
Paymaster General Geoffrey Robinson is forced to apologize to the House of Commons for a series of breaches of the House's rules on disclosure of outside financial interests. (→ December 23)

New York, 20
Vincent Van Gogh's *Portrait of the Artist without Beard* is sold for $71.5 million (£44 million) at Christie's, becoming the third most expensive painting ever.

London, 25
The Law Lords rule by a 3-2 majority that extradition proceedings can go ahead against former Chilean dictator Augusto Pinochet. Spain wants to try General Pinochet on charges of murder, torture, and genocide. (→ December 9)

London, 25
Jane Couch becomes the first woman to contest a professional boxing match in Britain, defeating Simone Lukic in the first round. Last year, Couch won a sexual discrimination case against the British Boxing Board of Control, which had denied her a professional licence.

Dublin, 26
Tony Blair becomes the first British prime minister to address the Irish parliament. He calls on them to "forgive and forget age-old enmities".

DEATHS
November 15. Kwame Ture, formerly known as Stokely Carmichael, Trinidad-born leader of the 1960s Black Power movement in the United States, dies in Guinea, West Africa, aged 57.

November 29. Robin Ray, broadcaster, entertainer, and popularizer of classical music, dies aged 65.

BRUSSELS, MONDAY 23

EU votes to lift beef export ban

European Union farm ministers voted this evening to lift the ban on the export of British beef imposed 32 months ago at the height of the scare over BSE, or "mad cow disease". Only the German minister voted against ending the ban.

Speaking for hard-pressed British farmers, Ben Gill of the National Farmers' Union said: "It is the best Christmas present we could have." The decision will not take effect immediately, however. Britain has first to complete a cull of potentially infected cattle, and EU inspectors will need to certify that British abattoirs satisfy stringent new conditions. The actual resumption of exports is expected to take place next spring.

The BSE crisis led to the slaughter of four million cattle and has cost taxpayers some £4 billion. The government acknowledges that it will be a long time before confidence in British beef is restored. (→ March 1)

KAZAKHSTAN, FRIDAY 20

Space station project takes off

The core module of the International Space Station in orbit around the Earth.

The biggest space project since the manned flights to the Moon got under way today when a Russian Proton rocket blasted off from Baikonur in Kazakhstan, carrying the first section of the International Space Station (ISS) into Earth orbit.

The ISS is a joint project by the United States, Russia, Japan, Canada, and nine European states, including Britain. It will take six years to complete, involving almost 100 rocket launches and 160 space walks.

The eventual cost of the ISS has been variously estimated at between £10 billion and £60 billion. The United States is expected to foot most of the bill. (→ May 31)

New York, Monday 16. Senator John Glenn and his wife, Annie, were treated to a ticker-tape parade through Manhattan today, celebrating the US senator's feat in crewing a space shuttle mission at the age of 77. The nine-day mission, aboard *Discovery*, has revived enthusiasm for the US space programme.

Cheers as Queen announces abolition of Lords

Lady Haden-Guest (left), better known as Jamie Lee Curtis, at the State Opening.

The State Opening of Parliament is an occasion that embodies all the idiosyncratic pageantry of the traditional British way of government. But today it saw the first shots fired in a constitutional revolution.

There were muffled cheers and murmurs of dissent as the Queen declared the government's intention to reform the House of Lords, removing "the right of hereditary peers to sit and vote" in Parliament.

Passions later flared in the House of Commons when Prime Minister Tony Blair spoke of his intention "to end the feudal domination of one half of our legislature" by Tory peers. Of the 759 hereditary lords whose seats are now at risk, only 18 support Labour. (→ December 3)

The Queen and Prince Philip arrive for the State Opening of Parliament, an occasion whose traditional ritual may soon face radical reform.

WESTMINSTER, MONDAY 30

Mandelson jibs at Hague's Rio jibe

A political storm has blown up over Tory leader William Hague's passing reference to Trade and Industry Secretary Peter Mandelson as "Lord Mandelson of Rio" in the House of Commons last week. The jibe was taken to refer to a story published in the satirical magazine *Punch*, falsely alleging that Mandelson toured gay venues in Rio de Janeiro with local British Council chief Martin Dowle.

The Tory leader has denied trying to make political capital out of rumours about Mandelson's sexuality, but Dowle accused Hague of using "innuendo, lies, and smears".

Birmingham, Monday 23. Sir Simon Rattle claimed the record for the world's largest orchestra today after conducting 3,503 young players in two performances of Arnold's *Little Suite No. 2*. The vast orchestra included 1,042 violinists, 551 flautists, and 377 trumpeters.

PARIS, WEDNESDAY 18

Victory for MI5 renegade Shayler

A French court today delivered a stinging rebuff to the British government by ruling that former MI5 officer David Shayler should not be extradited to face charges under the Official Secrets Act. Shayler had broken Britain's strict secrecy laws by leaking to the press embarrassing details of alleged MI5 incompetence and malpractice.

Accepting Shayler's argument that he was a victim of a political prosecution, the French court ordered his immediate release. At the prison gates, Shayler told the press that it was "a great day for justice".

Cranborne sacking rocks Tories

The Conservatives were in disarray today after party leader William Hague sacked the Tory leader in the House of Lords, Lord Cranborne.

The row exploded yesterday, after it emerged that Lord Cranborne had negotiated a deal with Labour over the planned abolition of the voting rights of hereditary peers. In return for an agreement by Labour to allow 91 of the 759 hereditary peers to stay in an interim chamber, the Tory peers would drop plans to obstruct government business.

This deal had not been authorized by Hague and, indeed, had been made without his knowledge.

Lord Cranborne told the press he had "been sacked for running in like an ill-trained spaniel". He accepted that he had "behaved outrageously" and had offered to resign, but Hague preferred to sack him. "If I was in his place," Lord Cranborne declared, "I would have done the same."

Other Tories took a less understanding view of Hague's action. Four Tory peers today resigned posts on the front bench. Ironically, the deal that Lord Cranborne negotiated seems sure to be adopted in spite of his dismissal, as it offers hereditary peers the only alternative to the total loss of their seats. (→ January 20)

Sacked Tory Lord Cranborne, who told Hague, "I have behaved outrageously."

London, Tuesday 1. The Turner Prize, Britain's most prestigious art award, has been won this year by Chris Ofili. The artist's paintings, some of which are made with dried elephant dung, were praised by the judges for their "originality and energy". (→ September 29)

Straw puts Pinochet in the dock

Home Secretary Jack Straw ruled today that extradition proceedings against General Augusto Pinochet, the former Chilean dictator, should be allowed to go ahead.

Pinochet was arrested in London in October after Spanish magistrates requested his extradition to face charges of torture, murder, and genocide. Last month the Law Lords ruled that Pinochet did not have immunity from extradition. The case now moves to British magistrates and could see several lengthy appeals before returning to the home secretary for the final surrender decision.

Straw's ruling was denounced by Tory leader William Hague as "cowardly" and by Baroness Thatcher, the former Tory prime minister, as a "shameful and damaging episode".

But Labour MPs applauded the home secretary's decision, and the human rights organization Amnesty International described it as "the birth of a new era for human rights".

Pinochet will make his first court appearance in south London tomorrow. He is currently living on an exclusive estate in Wentworth, Surrey. His stay there may now prove to be a lengthy one. (→ December 17)

IRAQ, THURSDAY 17

Desert Fox hammers Saddam

An American strike aircraft on board USS Enterprise, stationed in the Gulf, prepares to fly a night-time sortie against Iraq.

WASHINGTON, D.C., SATURDAY 19

Clinton impeached as air war rages

President Clinton's impeachment drives war off America's front pages.

The House of Representatives voted today to send President Bill Clinton for trial before the Senate on charges of perjury and obstruction of justice. A highly charged session on Capitol Hill saw Democrats walk out when they were not allowed to debate an option of censuring the president, and speaker-elect Bob Livingston shocked everyone by resigning over his own past sexual infidelities. Meanwhile, Clinton vowed to fight on until "the last hour of the last day" of his term. (→ January 12)

Last night the United States and Britain launched massive airstrikes against targets in Iraq. The aerial assault, code named "Desert Fox", is being delivered by American aircraft from the carrier *Enterprise*, British Tornados based in Kuwait, and Tomahawk cruise missiles launched both from ships and B-52 bombers.

In the United States, some opponents of President Bill Clinton have expressed cynicism about the timing of the onslaught, which coincides with the last stages in the political battle to impeach the president.

However, Clinton and his ally, British Prime Minister Tony Blair, claimed that the airstrikes were a necessary response to the obdurate behaviour of Iraqi dictator Saddam Hussein. The assault was triggered by a UN report stating that, despite repeated warnings, Saddam was still denying inspectors access to sites that might be used for the manufacture of weapons of mass destruction.

Describing Saddam as a "serial breaker of promises", Blair said there had been "no realistic alternative to military force." (→ December 22)

CHECHNYA, TUESDAY 8

Hostages executed when rescue bid goes awry

The severed heads of four Western hostages were today found in a sack on a roadside outside the Chechen capital, Grozny. The murdered men, Rudolf Petschi, Darren Hickey, and Peter Kennedy from Britain, and New Zealander Stan Shaw, were engineers employed by a British company to install a telephone network in Chechnya. Taken hostage by an armed Chechen gang three months ago, they were killed after Chechen security forces located and attacked the kidnappers.

Hollywood, Friday 18. *The Prince of Egypt*, **an animation by Steven Spielberg's DreamWorks group, opened worldwide tonight. Based on the story of Moses, it cost $100 m (£60 m) to make.**

JOHANNESBURG, WEDNESDAY 9

"Missing link" found in grotto

Dr Ron Clarke, a British scientist working in South Africa, today announced the discovery of the oldest complete skeleton and skull of a human ancestor. Dubbed Little Foot, the ape-like creature is estimated to have died around 3.6 million years ago. The remains were found in Silberberg Grotto, in the Sterkfontein caves outside Johannesburg.

S	M	T	W	T	F	S
		1	2	3	4	5
6	7	8	9	10	11	12
13	14	15	16	17	18	19
20	21	22	23	24	25	26
27	28	29	30	31		

Wimbledon, 22
The International Tennis Federation reveals that Czech tennis star Petr Korda failed a drug test during the 1998 Wimbledon tournament. However, the Federation accepted that Korda had been unaware of taking a prohibited substance.

Israel, 23
The Islamic militia Hizbollah fires salvos of Katyusha rockets into northern Israel from Lebanon, injuring 13 civilians. This follows an Israeli airstrike two days ago that killed a woman and six children in Lebanon's Bekaa Valley. (→ February 28)

Belgium, 23
Former Nato secretary-general Willy Claes is found guilty of corruption in a case relating to the award of defence contracts when he was a minister in the Belgian government in the 1980s.

Westminster, 27
In the wake of the resignation of Peter Mandelson, Prime Minister Tony Blair reaffirms his commitment to the New Labour policies with which Mandelson was closely identified. Blair states: "We got elected as New Labour, we'll govern as New Labour." (→ January 4)

Moscow, 29
Mikhail Gorbachev, the former leader of the Soviet Union, tells German magazine *Bunte* that he is broke after losing all his savings in a Russian bank collapse.

Munich, 29
Insurance consultants Munich Re Group report that large-scale natural disasters have become three times more common in the 1990s than they were in the 1960s.

City of London, 30
A surge on the London stock market leaves prices 15 per cent higher than at the start of the year, only three months after a crash that had analysts predicting worldwide recession.

London, 31
In the New Year's honours list, former prime minister John Major is made a Companion of Honour for his role in the Northern Ireland peace process. Other awards include knighthoods for Formula One racing's Frank Williams and for actor Nigel Hawthorne.

DEATHS
December 22. Lord Donald Soper, Methodist preacher, pacifist, and socialist campaigner, dies aged 95.

HAWAII, FRIDAY 25

Branson balloon bid fails again

There was no happy Christmas for Virgin boss Richard Branson, as his third attempt to fly a balloon non-stop around the world ended in the Pacific Ocean near Hawaii.

The ICO *Global Challenger* took off from Marrakesh in Morocco on December 18, crewed by Branson, American millionaire Steve Fossett, and Per Lindstrand. The flight had to deviate from its planned course to avoid the war zone over Iraq, and was then refused permission to cross China. At the last minute, however, the Chinese authorities reversed their decision and the balloon flew on to the Pacific.

It was a severe disappointment for the balloonists when they then encountered adverse weather conditions and were forced to ditch in the ocean. After a hazardous landing, they were plucked from the sea by Hawaiian coastguard helicopters.

Branson said that he was "very sorry to have let people down". He added: "We really thought we had it in our grasp." (→ March 1)

Richard Branson (centre) and his co-pilots pose in front of their balloon before lifting off.

Melbourne, Tuesday 29. In a dramatic end to the fourth Test of the Ashes series, England snatched victory away from Australia. Darren Gough (left) took the final wicket for a 12-run win. (→ January 5)

THE GULF, TUESDAY 22

"Ramadan gift" bomb is no joke for Muslims

The four-day campaign of American and British airstrikes against Iraq, code named "Desert Fox", ended abruptly last Saturday, the first day of the Muslim holy month of Ramadan. Western leaders feared that continuing the attacks on an Islamic country in Ramadan might alienate pro-Western Muslims.

Efforts to manage Islamic sensibilities have been undermined, however, by a press photograph. It shows a message scrawled by a US serviceman on the side of a bomb, reading: "Here's a Ramadan present from Chad Rickenberg." Muslims have not been amused.

WESTMINSTER, WEDNESDAY 23

Ministers quit after home loan row

Peter Mandelson, one of the prime architects of New Labour, leaving his Notting Hill home.

Trade and Industry Secretary Peter Mandelson, one of Prime Minister Tony Blair's closest associates, today resigned from the government after being criticized over his financial relationship with Geoffrey Robinson, the paymaster general.

At the start of the week, details emerged of a £373,000 loan made by Robinson to Mandelson in 1996. It enabled Mandelson, then a back-bench MP, to buy a four-storey house in fashionable Notting Hill.

Mandelson denied that he had done anything wrong in "accepting a loan from a friend and fellow MP". But questions were raised over his failure to reveal the existence of the loan when he became trade and industry secretary last July, especially since his department then got involved in an investigation of Robinson's business affairs.

Although he denied any wrong-doing, Mandelson said he had felt obliged to resign "to restore people's faith in this government, their confidence in ministers, and also their regard for my own integrity".

Robinson, a millionaire brought into the government to liaise with business, also resigned, blaming recent attacks he had endured over his financial dealings. (→ December 27)

Britain, Monday 21. Furby, an "interactive pet" that answers back when spoken to, has been the hottest present for children this Christmas. As toy shops have sold out, desperate parents have paid up to £600 for a Furby on the black market.

SYDNEY, MONDAY 28

Tragedy as storm hits prestigious ocean yacht race

Rescuers are still searching the ocean for survivors after yachts contesting the annual Sydney-Hobart race ran into treacherously high winds and heavy seas off Flinders Island in Bass Strait. Two yachtsmen are known to have died and four others are missing, including a British Olympic yachtsman, 33-year-old Glyn Charles, from Emsworth, Hampshire, who was aboard the yacht *Sword of Orion*. This is the worst disaster in the yacht race's 54-year history.

YEMEN, TUESDAY 29

Four hostages killed during rescue attempt

Four tourists, three of them British and one Australian, have died after being kidnapped by Islamic rebels in Yemen. Margaret Whitehouse, Ruth Williamson, and Peter Rowe, as well as Australian Andrew Thirsk, were killed when Yemeni forces stormed the kidnappers' hideout. Twelve other captives, including nine Britons, were freed.

The kidnapping took place on Monday, when the convoy carrying the tourists through the Yemeni countryside was ambushed by an armed band. A British embassy official in Yemen said that the survivors were "in a state of severe shock".

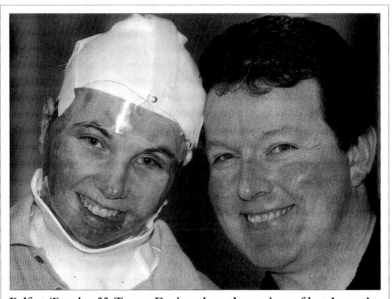

Belfast, Tuesday 22. Tracey Devine, the only survivor of last August's Omagh bombing still in hospital, has been allowed to go home for Christmas. Tracey and her husband Paul (right) lost their 18-month-old daughter in the blast. The bomb killed 29 people. (→ August 15)

FORT WILLIAM, WEDNESDAY 30

Drama of death and survival on Aonach Mor

Three people have survived and four have died after an avalanche struck a party of climbers on Aonach Mor peak in the Scottish Highlands. After 16 hours of being buried under tons of snow, Steven Newton, Sarah Finch, and Roger Wilde were finally discovered by rescuers last night. They were suffering from hypothermia, but were otherwise uninjured.

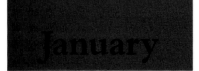

S	M	T	W	T	F	S
					1	2
3	4	5	6	7	8	9
10	11	12	13	14	15	16
17	18	19	20	21	22	23
24	25	26	27	28	29	30
31						

Pakistan, 3
A bomb meant for Pakistan Prime Minister Nawaz Sharif kills three people on a road near Lahore. Officials suspect that a terrorist group called the MQM is responsible. (→ October 12)

Sydney, 5
Australia's cricketers beat England by 98 runs in the fifth and final Test of the Ashes series. England lose the series 3-1.

London, 6
London has its hottest January day since 1841, with the temperature rising as high as 15.7°C (60°F).

Britain, 7
A 25-year study claims that using the contraceptive pill has no adverse long-term effects on women's health.

City of London, 7
The Bank of England monetary policy committee trims interest rates for the fourth consecutive month, from 6.25 to 6 per cent. (→ February 4)

Los Angeles, 10
The Walt Disney Company recalls more than three million copies of a children's cartoon video, *The Rescuers*, because of unspecified objectionable images spotted in two of its 110,000 frames.

London, 12
The Police Complaints Authority says that none of the officers involved in the Stephen Lawrence murder case was guilty of racism. Only one officer, Detective Inspector Ben Bullock, is to face disciplinary charges. (→ February 22)

Washington, D.C., 12
Bill Clinton pays Paula Jones $850,000 (£520,000) to settle her sexual harassment suit against him. (→ January 14)

Britain, 13
Official figures show that unemployment in December fell to 1.31 million, the lowest level since 1980. (→ February 17)

London, 15
Model Jerry Hall files for divorce from Rolling Stone Mick Jagger after eight years of marriage. (→ January 18)

DEATHS
January 10. Brian Moore, Belfast-born Canadian novelist and scriptwriter, dies in California, aged 77.

January 11. Naomi Mitchison, Scottish feminist and author, dies aged 101.

BRUSSELS, THURSDAY 14

Euro leaders accused of fraud and nepotism

The European parliament today voted to keep the European Commission, Europe's executive body, in place despite allegations of fraud, maladministration, and nepotism. Pauline Green, leader of the parliament's largest group, the Socialists, said that the president of the commission, Jacques Santer, had agreed to a list of concessions prior to the vote. These included setting up a committee, appointed by both parliament and the commission, that would investigate the allegations.

The political crisis erupted only a few days after the launch of the euro, Europe's new monetary unit. Paul van Buitenen, an auditor for the commission, released information detailing acts of fraud by individual commissioners. President Santer in turn suspended van Buitenen on half pay and declared that he would not force any commissioner to resign.

The main allegations focus on two commissioners, Edith Cresson of France and Manuel Marin of Spain, but four other commissioners are also cited as having acted irresponsibly and negligently. Santer's compromise with the Socialists in parliament has averted, temporarily, the worst political crisis in the EU's brief history. (→ March 16)

CAPE TOWN, FRIDAY 8

Shots fired during anti-Blair protest

Prime Minister Tony Blair's first visit to South Africa was today marred by violence as fighting broke out between security forces and Muslim protesters in Cape Town.

The heated demonstration was reportedly organized by a group called Muslims Against Global Oppression, and was in protest at Britain's role in airstrikes on Iraq.

Protesters chanting "Death to Tony Blair" gathered outside Cape Town's castle, where the prime minister was handing out medals to British soldiers for their part in retraining South Africa's armed forces. Police reportedly opened fire after spotting guns being handled by protesters. They fired birdshot from shotguns, wounding three people.

Muslim protesters in Cape Town express their hostility to the prime minister's visit.

WESTMINSTER, MONDAY 4

Chancellor's spin doctor to resign

Charlie Whelan, press secretary to Chancellor of the Exchequer Gordon Brown, announced today that he will leave his post after allegations that he was responsible for leaking the "home loan" revelation that led to the downfall of former Trade and Industry Secretary Peter Mandelson. Whelan denied that he was behind the leak, but said the media furore was making it impossible for him to do his job. Political commentators are suggesting that the whole "home loan" affair is part of an ongoing feud between the chancellor and Prime Minister Tony Blair — Mandelson is one of Blair's closest political allies. (→ October 11)

JERUSALEM, THURSDAY 14

Israeli Miss World speaks out about rape ordeal

Linor Abargil is mobbed after winning the Miss World title in the Seychelles in November.

Nineteen-year-old Linor Abargil, the Israeli beauty queen who won last year's Miss World pageant, today confirmed rumours that she had been raped at knifepoint. The sexual assault allegedly took place in early October, less than two months before her Miss World triumph.

Abargil's statement read: "Women who are assaulted must react to the crimes committed against them … so that these incidents do not become an accepted routine part of our lives." Her stance, welcomed by Israeli women's groups, has angered many Jewish fundamentalists who were already outraged by Abargil's participation in beauty contests.

WESTMINSTER, SUNDAY 10
Cook's wife tells of troubled marriage, lovers, and drink

Prime Minister Tony Blair sprang to the defence of his foreign secretary, Robin Cook, today as the *Sunday Times* began serial publication of the much-publicized memoirs of Cook's ex-wife, Margaret.

The memoirs portray Cook as a serial adulterer who had at least six affairs during the 28-year marriage. Margaret Cook also alleges that he had a serious drink problem in the 1980s and was once "flat out on the dining-room floor with a brandy bottle". Cook left his wife in 1997 when a newspaper found out about his affair with his secretary, Gaynor Regan, whom he has since married.

Speaking on BBC1's *Breakfast with Frost* this morning, Tony Blair praised the foreign secretary for doing "a superb job on behalf of the government and the country". He called on the media to concentrate on the "things that really matter" rather than on "scandal and gossip and trivia".

Chicago, Tuesday 12. The world's highest-paid athlete, basketball player Michael Jordan, who helped the Chicago Bulls win the NBA title six times, today announced his retirement.

LONDON, WEDNESDAY 6
Prince Edward finds his princess

Sophie Rhys-Jones and Prince Edward after the announcement of their engagement.

Prince Edward, 34, the youngest son of the Queen and seventh in line to the throne, is to marry a 33-year-old public relations executive, Sophie Rhys-Jones. The couple have been courting for five years.

A date for the marriage has not yet been fixed, but the prince has already made it clear that he intends to have a low-key family wedding, rather than a lavish royal ceremony like those of his brothers.

The couple are acutely aware of the need for theirs to be a successful royal marriage. The prince said he and Rhys-Jones were "the very best of friends" who "also happen to love each other". (→ May 27)

WASHINGTON, D.C., THUR. 14
Clinton goes on trial but his popularity soars

Today the prosecution opened its case in the Senate trial of President Bill Clinton, who is charged with perjury and attempted obstruction of justice.

The charges, arising out of the Lewinsky affair, could see the president removed from office. But the US is more bored than awed by the proceedings. Major TV networks are providing only limited coverage.

Polls show Clinton's popularity soaring, with more than 60 per cent approving his presidency. Few people believe vote-conscious senators will defy the mood of electors by finding Clinton guilty. (→ February 6)

Switzerland, Tuesday 5. Prince Harry, while on a skiing holiday in the Swiss Alps, displayed his skill at snowblading, the latest winter sports craze.

BRUSSELS, FRIDAY 1
Euro launch heralds new era

At midnight last night, 11 of the 15 member states of the European Union celebrated the start of a new era of monetary union. Their official unit of currency is now the euro, although their national currencies such as the French franc, the Italian lira, and the German deutschmark will continue in everyday use for another three years. At the launch in Brussels, Italian Finance Minister Carlo Ciampi confirmed the worst fears of British Eurosceptics by describing monetary union as "a decisive step towards the ever closer political union of Europe".

The British government has so far failed to make a definite commitment to monetary union. But with the new euro bloc embracing over 300 million people and responsible for a fifth of world economic output, pressure on Britain to join may prove irresistible. (→ February 23)

S	M	T	W	T	F	S
					1	2
3	4	5	6	7	8	9
10	11	12	13	14	15	16
17	18	19	20	21	22	23
24	25	26	27	28	29	30
31						

Serbia, 18
Serb authorities refuse to allow war crimes prosecutor Louise Arbour to enter Kosovo where she is to investigate the Recak massacre. (→ February 4)

South Africa, 18
The West Indies lose a cricket Test series against South Africa 5-0. It is the first time that a West Indian cricket team has lost every match in a series.

Old Bailey, 19
In the Central Criminal Court, former Tory MP and Cabinet minister Jonathan Aitken admits perjury and intending to pervert the course of justice. The offences took place during a libel action against *The Guardian* in 1997. (→ June 8)

Westminster, 20
The government sets up a Royal Commission, chaired by Lord Wakeham, to report on proposals for a new second chamber of Parliament to replace the House of Lords. (→ August 24)

Villa Park, 22
In a FA Cup fourth-round upset, Second Division leaders Fulham, managed by Kevin Keegan, beat Premier League club Aston Villa 0-2. (→ February 17)

Westminster, 25
MPs vote to lower the age of consent for gay sex to 16. The bill will face resistance in the House of Lords. (→ April 13)

Iraq, 25
An American aircraft flying a mission against Iraqi air defence installations mistakenly fires a missile into a residential area in Basra, killing 11 civilians.

Westminster, 25
Home Secretary Jack Straw says teenage mothers should be encouraged to view the offering of their babies for adoption as "a positive, responsible choice".

Northern Ireland, 27
IRA defector Eamon Collins is murdered in south Armagh. The murder reinforces calls for the government to suspend the early release of terrorists. (→ March 15)

Andover, 27
Circus trainer Mary Chipperfield is found guilty of cruelty to a chimpanzee on a farm in Hampshire. (→ April 9)

Strasbourg, 31
Tory Euro-MP Tom Spencer resigns after Heathrow customs officers find drugs and pornography in his bag.

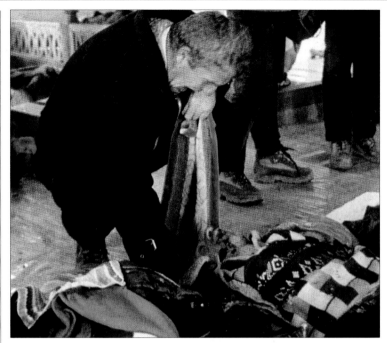
Ethnic Albanians mourn their dead, laid out on the floor of Recak's village mosque.

BRUSSELS, SUNDAY 17
Massacre in Kosovo brings call to arms

The massacre of 45 ethnic Albanians by Serb forces in the Kosovan village of Recak last Friday has reopened the possibility of Nato airstrikes against Serbia. Nato Secretary-General Javier Solana today described the killings as "a flagrant violation of international humanitarian law".

Airstrikes were narrowly averted last October, when Serbia accepted a deal intended to end its war with Kosovan independence fighters. Now Nato is again threatening military action unless Serbia halts the ethnic cleansing and allows those responsible to be prosecuted by the international war crimes tribunal. (→ January 18)

LAUSANNE, SUNDAY 24
Bribery scandal rocks Olympics

Six members of the International Olympic Committee (IOC), the body that runs the Olympic games, are to be expelled after allegations of bribery and corruption. Three other IOC members have already resigned.

It is alleged that Salt Lake City in effect bought the votes of IOC members with gifts worth a total of £500,000 in order to ensure that its bid to host the 2002 Winter Olympics would be successful.

The IOC president, Juan Antonio Samaranch, is resisting pressure to resign. He is due to retire in 2001.

BIRMINGHAM, MONDAY 25
Strangers marry in "love experiment"

Model Carla Germaine, 23, and sales manager Greg Cordell, 28, met for the first time today – and married. Described as "a scientific experiment in love", the marriage was organized by BRMB, a Birmingham local radio station. But the couple denied they were simply parties to a media stunt. "Everyone expects us to split up", Mr Cordell said, "but we're going to prove them wrong." (→ April 14)

London, Thursday 28. When leaving a party at the Ritz this evening Prince Charles and Camilla Parker-Bowles appeared together in front of press cameras for the first time in their 20-year friendship.

Ashdown resigns as Lib Dem leader

Paddy Ashdown and his wife, Jane, who complained that his family "never see him".

Paddy Ashdown, leader of the Liberal Democrats for the last 11 years, announced today that he will step down this summer. Explaining his decision, Ashdown said: "I always wanted to go at a time when people were saying 'Why is he going?' rather than 'Why isn't he going?'"

Ashdown's wife, Jane, made it clear that she had wanted him to quit for family reasons. "We never see the kids, never see each other," she said. Ashdown agreed that it had been a "very personal" decision.

When Ashdown took control of the Liberal Democrats in 1988, the party had the support of a mere 5 per cent of voters. He leaves it with 46 MPs, the strongest Liberal representation since 1929. (→ August 9)

Thousands dead in Colombian earthquake

The death toll is rising in the aftermath of the earthquake disaster that struck the South American state of Colombia at lunchtime on Monday. Original estimates of a few hundred dead have been rapidly revised upwards to thousands.

Registering 6.0 on the Richter scale, the earthquake devastated five provinces in mountainous western Colombia, an area mostly devoted to coffee plantations. About 20 towns and cities are thought to be badly affected. The authorities admit they still know nothing of what has happened in remote villages.

Armenia, a provincial capital with a population of 300,000, felt the full force of the quake. Entire neighbourhoods were reduced to rubble. Electricity and water have been cut off, and the basketball court at the city's university has been turned into a makeshift morgue.

Earth-moving equipment has been slow to arrive, and people have been digging through the rubble with sticks or their bare hands in the search for survivors. Heavy rain has hampered the rescue effort. Armenia's mayor, Alvaro Patino, said on radio: "We need everything – food, medicines, blood, blankets …" Colombia's president, Andres Pastrana Arango, has appealed for international aid.

A survivor of the Colombian earthquake stands amid the ruins of her home town.

Jagger says Hall was never truly his wife

Model Jerry Hall, who has filed for divorce.

Lawyers acting for 55-year-old rock star Mick Jagger today responded to a divorce petition, filed by model Jerry Hall last week, with the claim that the couple "are not, and never have been, married".

Jagger and Hall have been together for 21 years and have four children. They married in a six-hour Hindu ceremony on a beach in Bali in 1990. But the legal status of this ceremony is now in doubt. Hall is said to be seeking £30 million, which would be the largest divorce settlement ever. (→ August 13)

AIDS "traced back to monkey meat"

Scientists believe they have traced the source of the HIV virus that causes AIDS. A team led by Beatrice Hahn of the University of Alabama has identified the virus HIV-1 in a species of West African chimpanzee.

The scientists speculate that the virus could have been transferred to humans when hunters killing the animals for food were contaminated with chimpanzee blood. More than 30 million people worldwide are infected with the HIV virus.

Westminster, 1
The government announces a 4.7 per cent rise in basic pay for nurses, with a 12 per cent rise for junior nurses.

Brussels, 1
A European Commission report says that cars cost more in Britain than in any other major European country.

Britain, 1
Church spokesmen attack plans for a Yorkshire TV documentary called *Birth Race 2000*, covering couples likely to have a baby next January 1. YTV hopes to broadcast a "millennium birth" live.

Chester, 2
Jenny Cupit, 24-year-old mother of two, is sentenced to life imprisonment for killing deputy headmistress Kathryn Linaker, the wife of a man with whom she was having an affair.

Glasgow, 3
Scientists at Glasgow University report that flavonols, antioxidants found in fruits and vegetables, are the key to preventing heart disease and many other serious ailments. They recommend lollo rosso lettuce, cherry tomatoes, and Chilean Cabernet Sauvignon.

Northern Ireland, 3
The human rights organization Amnesty International announces that it is to investigate "punishment beatings" carried out by paramilitary groups in Northern Ireland.

City of London, 4
The Bank of England cuts the base rate from 6 per cent to 5.5 per cent, the lowest level in four years. (→ June 10)

Outer Space, 4
Cosmonauts on board the Russian *Mir* space station fail to deploy a giant mirror that would have brought light to part of Siberia during the long winter nights.

Maryland, 5
Boxer Mike Tyson is sentenced to 12 months in prison for attacking two men after a traffic accident.

Exeter, 5
Speaking at Exeter University, Chief Inspector of Schools Chris Woodhead says that sex between a teacher and a pupil can sometimes be an "educative" experience. (→ March 6)

DEATHS
February 2. Paul Mellon, American philanthropist, dies aged 91.

Lewinsky takes the stand as Clinton trial falters

In a demure black outfit and pearls, Monica Lewinsky takes the oath before testifying.

"For the first time, the Senate and the people of the United States of America are going to get a chance to meet Monica Lewinsky, the person." Thus Representative James Rogan, a prosecutor in the trial of President Bill Clinton, introduced the showing of excerpts from Lewinsky's six-hour testimony, videoed in a Washington hotel suite earlier in the week.

It was indeed the first time that Americans had seen Lewinsky speak, but like the rest of the Senate trial, the occasion failed to catch fire. Sober, sad, and sentimental, she produced no revelations or sensations about her affair with the president.

Republicans hoped that drumming up sympathy for Lewinsky as a victim of the president might revive the prosecution. But it seems that most senators, like most Americans, just want to bring the case to a close as soon as possible. (→ February 12)

LONDON, WEDNESDAY 3
"Airtours 12" accused of air rage

Twelve passengers on an Airtours flight to Jamaica last Sunday were allegedly so disruptive that the pilot made an emergency landing at Norfolk, Virginia, to throw them off the plane. The "Airtours 12" arrived at Heathrow today after paying for their own flights home. Described by air staff as drunken brawling, the event was dismissed by the 12 as "just a sing song". It has triggered a debate about violence on board aircraft, dubbed "air rage" in the press.

BELGRADE, THURSDAY 4
Serb peace vote raises hopes

The parliament of Serbia has voted to send a delegation to peace talks with ethnic Albanian leaders from Serb-ruled Kosovo. The talks will be held at Rambouillet, France. The Western powers are pressuring both sides to accept a deal giving Kosovo limited autonomy. But Serbia has rejected plans for an international peacekeeping force. (→ February 7)

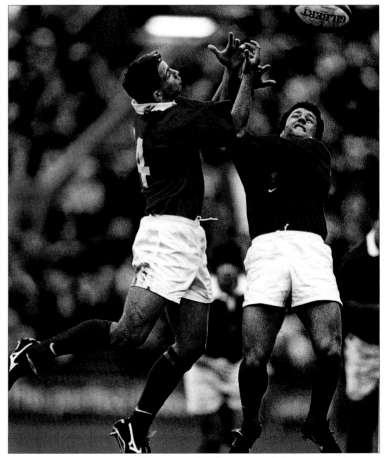

Lansdowne Road, Saturday 6. On the first day of the Five Nations Championship, Ireland nearly beat reigning champions France, but lost 9–10 due to a last-minute penalty kick. (→ March 6)

LONDON, TUESDAY 2

England boss Hoddle sacked

Judge sends killer nanny home

Australian nanny Louise Sullivan.

An Old Bailey judge ruled today that a nanny who shook a baby to death should be free to return to her native Australia. Louise Sullivan, aged 27, killed six-month-old Caroline Jongen in April 1997. Judge Mitchell said that a thyroid disorder had made her mentally deficient and "wholly unsuitable" to be a nanny. Taking the view that she needed treatment rather than punishment, he said: "No sentence imposed on you can mend the pain of the parents."

Glenn Hoddle is shown the door by the Football Association after controversial remarks about reincarnation and the disabled.

England football manager Glenn Hoddle had his £350,000-a-year contract terminated today after remarks he made about the disabled caused widespread outrage.

Hoddle's downfall began with an interview published in *The Times* at the end of January in which he expressed his views on reincarnation. According to the interviewer, Matt Dickinson, Hoddle said: "You and I have been physically given two hands and two legs and half-decent brains. Some people have not been born like that for a reason. The karma is working from another lifetime." *The Times* ran the story under the heading: "Hoddle says disabled are paying price of sin."

The England manager strongly rejected this interpretation of his remarks, but subsequent interviews in which he reiterated his belief in reincarnation failed to allay criticism.

Hoddle's position was weakened by poor results in England's matches since the 1998 World Cup finals, and by reports of differences between the manager and key England players. Hoddle had also been ridiculed for attaching faith healer Eileen Drewery to the England squad.

The FA said today that their decision to sack Hoddle had been taken "with regret", but the situation had become untenable. Hoddle accepted that he had made "a serious error of judgement" and apologized for any pain he had inadvertently caused.

Former Leeds manager Howard Wilkinson has been appointed caretaker manager. (→ February 17)

Britain, Monday 1. *Shakespeare in Love*, starring Joseph Fiennes, has taken a record-breaking £1.82 million at cinemas on its opening weekend. (→ March 21)

S	M	T	W	T	F	S
	1	2	3	4	5	6
7	8	9	10	11	12	13
14	15	16	17	18	19	20
21	22	23	24	25	26	27
28						

France, 7
Representatives of Serbia and ethnic Albanian groups from Kosovo meet for peace talks in Rambouillet chateau, in the Paris suburbs. (→ February 14)

Delhi, 7
In a Test match between India and Pakistan, Indian leg-spin bowler Anil Kumble takes ten wickets in an innings. It is only the second time this feat has been achieved in a Test.

Old Bailey, 8
Britain's first war crimes trial opens in the Central Criminal Court. Anthony Sawoniuk, aged 77, is charged with the murder of Jews in his native Belarus during the Nazi holocaust. (→ April 1)

Vatican, 8
A Vatican inquiry into the murder of the newly appointed head of the Papal Swiss Guard, Alois Estermann, and his wife last May concludes that their killer, Cedric Tornay, acted "in a fit of madness" under the influence of cannabis. Tornay killed himself after the double murder.

Westminster, 9
Home Secretary Jack Straw tells MPs that the police are not doing enough to recruit officers from ethnic minorities. He sets a minimum target of 7 per cent ethnic minority officers. (→ April 14)

Chamonix, 9
An avalanche strikes the hamlet of Le Tour in the French Alps, killing ten people. (→ February 25)

Rome, 10
The Court of Cassation, Italy's highest court, rules that a woman cannot be raped if she is wearing tight denim jeans, since they cannot be removed without her cooperation. In protest, women MPs wear jeans in the Italian parliament.

Britain, 12
A group of scientists calls for a five-year moratorium on new genetically modified (GM) foods as public concern about their effect on health grows. The government says that fears about GM foods are ill-founded. (→ February 18)

DEATHS

February 8. Iris Murdoch, author of novels such as *Under the Net, The Bell*, and *The Sea, The Sea*, dies aged 79 after succumbing to Alzheimer's disease.

February 9. Bryan Mosley, the actor who played Alf Roberts in *Coronation Street*, dies in Bradford aged 67.

Highbury, Saturday 13. Arsenal coach Arsene Wenger has offered to replay today's FA Cup tie against Sheffield United after his side won due to an "ungentlemanly" goal. Referee Peter Jones (right) allowed the goal scored when the Sheffield players were expecting the ball returned to them after an injury stoppage. (→ February 23)

LONDON, THURSDAY 11
Vanessa on the defensive after "phoney guest" revelations

Vanessa Feltz described the revelations about fake guests as "horrifying".

The BBC confirmed today that some guests who have appeared on a confessional talk show hosted by Vanessa Feltz were in fact actors masquerading as "ordinary people". Three people have been suspended while the BBC conducts an inquiry.

Since the launch of *The Vanessa Show* last month, there have been at least four phoney guests. In one case, two "sisters" who appeared in a programme on sibling rivalry were in fact striptease artistes who had never met. A "battered wife" who appeared in another episode of the show was an unmarried actress.

The case reveals the pressure on programme makers to satisfy demand for sensational "real-life" material. Last week, Channel 4 had to apologize for a documentary on rent-boys in which the "clients" were fake. The BBC said today: "Audiences must be able to believe in the integrity of our programmes." (→ June 9)

WASHINGTON, D.C., FRIDAY 12
Clinton escapes in flat finale to "Monicagate"

The impeachment trial of President Bill Clinton ended today with a more decisive acquittal than his most dedicated supporters had hoped for.

His prosecutors not only failed to achieve the two-thirds majority they needed in the Senate to convict the president, but also fell short of a simple majority. The Senate found Clinton not guilty of perjury by 55 to 45. On the charge of obstruction of justice, they split 50-50.

A relieved president emerged from the White House to appeal for "a time of national reconciliation and renewal". Carefully avoiding any hint of triumph, he again proclaimed himself "profoundly sorry" for the deeds that had led to the trial.

But many Republicans were unrepentant about their pursuit of the president over the Lewinsky affair. Senator Robert Bennett said that Clinton would go down in history as "the most polished liar we have ever had in the White House". (→ July 29)

United States, Wednesday 10. Teletubby Tinky Winky has been denounced by American Baptist preacher Jerry Falwell as a "gay role model". Falwell claims that Tinky Winky is a boy, yet carries a red purse and wears purple, "the colour of gay pride".

Hussein mourned as statesman and peacemaker

King Hussein of Jordan, an influential player on the world stage for half a century.

King Hussein of Jordan was buried today in his capital city, Amman, at a funeral attended by more than 50 world leaders. The 63-year-old monarch died on Sunday after a long battle against cancer. Openly distraught with grief, Jordanians lined the streets to watch the funeral cortège. Flanked by Bedouin guards, the coffin was followed by the late king's favourite white stallion, Amr.

Educated in Britain, King Hussein came to the throne in 1952. He led his country into a disastrous war with Israel in 1967, and in 1970 used his Bedouin troops to drive the Palestine Liberation Organization (PLO) out of Jordan – a move that, at the time, earned him the hostility of many Arabs. In his later years, however, he emerged as a leading player in the Middle East peace process. UN Secretary-General Kofi Annan spoke yesterday of the late king's "lifelong struggle to bring peace to the ordinary men and women of the Middle East".

King Hussein was married four times and had 11 children. During his lengthy illness, a struggle over the succession broke out within the Hashemite ruling family. Only two weeks ago, King Hussein removed his brother Prince Hassan as heir to the throne – a position he had held for 34 years – replacing him with the king's eldest son, Abdullah, who now becomes King Abdullah II.

King Hussein's coffin, draped in the Jordanian national flag, is escorted by members of his Bedouin royal guard.

Enemies rub shoulders at Hussein "funeral summit"

Mourners at the funeral included President Clinton, as well as three former US presidents.

Hailed as a peacemaker during his lifetime, King Hussein also achieved a remarkable symbolic mingling of declared enemies at his funeral.

British Prime Minister Tony Blair, US President Bill Clinton, and three former US presidents – Jimmy Carter, George Bush, and Gerald Ford – found themselves rubbing shoulders with senior representatives of Iraq, Libya, and Sudan, all countries that have been attacked by Western missiles. Palestinian leader Yassir Arafat and Syrian President Hafez Assad were there alongside an Israeli delegation, led by Prime Minister Binyamin Netanyahu. The presence of Assad, whose country is still officially at war with Israel, was seen as especially significant.

Diplomatic correspondents spoke of a "funeral summit" as talks were held behind closed doors in Amman hotels. In a region split by bitter conflicts, the presence of such traditionally hostile figures side by side marked a major step towards peace.

S	M	T	W	T	F	S
	1	2	3	4	5	6
7	8	9	10	11	12	13
14	15	16	17	18	19	20
21	22	23	24	25	26	27
28						

France, 14
Serb representatives at the Rambouillet peace talks are told that if by the end of the week they do not agree to a Nato peace plan giving autonomy to Kosovo, they will face airstrikes. (→ February 20)

Birmingham, 14
At the Bupa Indoor Grand Prix event, Ethiopian runner Haile Gebrselassie sets a new world record for the 5,000 m with a time of 12 minutes 50.38 seconds.

Sudan, 14
An independent report says that a factory in Sudan destroyed by US missiles last August was producing pharmaceutical products, not chemical weapons as the American government claimed.

Westminster, 15
Home Secretary Jack Straw proposes that people with personality disorders that make them a danger to others should be liable to be detained indefinitely, even if they have not committed any crime.

Berlin, 16
The German government announces that it is setting up a fund to compensate people who worked as slave labourers under the Nazi regime in World War II.

Spain, 17
Two British pilots, Andy Elson and Colin Prescot, launch another bid to fly around the globe by balloon. Their Cable and Wireless craft takes off from Almeria, on the southern coast of Spain. (→ March 7)

Vatican, 18
It is reported that the Pope has asked Britain to allow General Pinochet to return to Chile. (→ March 24)

London, 18
The Kurdish occupation of the Greek embassy in London ends peacefully. Protester Nejla Kanteper is recovering in hospital from her burns. (→ March 15)

London, 18
Former MP Matthew Parris reveals that celebrity guests appearing on *Countdown*, featuring Carol Vorderman, are prompted with answers through hidden earpieces.

London, 19
Spice Girl Melanie Brown gives birth to a daughter, who is named Phoenix.

DEATHS
February 15. John Ehrlichman, former adviser to President Richard Nixon and jailed in 1974 for his part in the Watergate cover-up, dies aged 73.

Public outcry over GM foods

A label identifying the contents of the tin as having been genetically modified.

The government has been forced into an embarrassing U-turn over genetically modified (GM) foods, made from plants that have been "improved" by genetic engineering.

Three days ago, Prime Minister Tony Blair publicly endorsed GM foods, saying they were safe and that he ate them himself. Today, however, bowing to public pressure, the government said that the commercial growing of GM crops would not be allowed in Britain until further trials had proved they were not harmful.

The food scare began when some scientists revived previously scorned research showing that GM foods could harm the immune systems of rats. When it emerged that some human genes were being grafted into plants, the press dubbed the products "Frankenstein foods". Environmental campaigners joined in, claiming that GM crops could harm wildlife.

The credibility of the government's original defence of GM foods was not helped by the fact that the science minister, Lord Sainsbury, has business interests in GM products.

Supermarkets are rushing to clear their shelves of products containing GM ingredients, despite most scientists arguing that GM foods can bring huge benefits and have no proven harmful effects. (→ May 18)

Bombers on alert as talks go to the brink

The peace talks on the future of the Serbian province of Kosovo being held at Rambouillet reached a critical point today. Nato has said it will launch airstrikes against Serbia if the Serbs refuse to allow Nato forces into Kosovo to police an autonomy deal. But a deadline for agreement, set for noon today, was allowed to pass without military action.

Embassy staff from Nato countries have been withdrawn from Serbia and Nato aircraft have been placed in readiness. But the Serbs appear to be gambling on Nato lacking the will to start a war. (→ February 23)

London, Wednesday 17. Kevin Keegan today agreed to become England soccer manager, but for four matches only. He insists on keeping his present job at Second Division Fulham. (→ March 27)

New Deal hailed as unemployment falls

The government claimed today that the latest employment statistics prove its "New Deal", designed to get the young jobless into work, is having a real effect. Contrary to gloomy predictions by economic experts, unemployment has fallen to its lowest level since June 1980. The figures for youth unemployment are even more impressive, down by 52 per cent since May 1997.

London, Monday 15. Radio One presenter Zoe Ball announced today that she is to marry Norman Cook, better known as the dance DJ Fatboy Slim.

Robbie Williams tops Brit Awards

The Brit Awards, the annual pop music jamboree, was this year a triumph for former Take That singer Robbie Williams, who walked off with three trophies, for best male singer, best single ("Angels"), and best video ("Millennium").

A more serious note was struck by appeals on behalf of a campaign to cancel the debts of developing countries. Former boxer Muhammad Ali appeared alongside U2 singer Bono to promote the campaign.

Kurds rage as leader is seized

North London schoolgirl Nejla Kanteper shows the strength of her feelings by setting herself on fire.

Kurdish protesters have occupied Greek embassies in 20 cities across the world, in response to the arrest of Kurdish rebel leader Abdullah Ocalan. Wanted by the Turkish authorities for fomenting an armed uprising in eastern Turkey, Ocalan had taken refuge in the Greek embassy in Nairobi. He was seized by Turkish agents when he left the embassy on Monday, and was flown back to Turkey to stand trial.

The Kurds turned their fury on the Greeks, thought to have betrayed Ocalan, and on the Israelis, believed to be Turkey's accomplices. In London yesterday 15-year-old Nejla Kanteper set herself on fire in front of the Greek embassy. In Berlin, three Kurdish protesters were shot dead today trying to break into the Israeli consulate. The wave of protest is not yet spent. (→ February 18)

Kurdish leader Ocalan with his abductors – they said: "Welcome back to your country."

S	M	T	W	T	F	S
	1	2	3	4	5	6
7	8	9	10	11	12	13
14	15	16	17	18	19	20
21	22	23	24	25	26	27
28						

Manchester, 22
Family doctor Harold Shipman, charged last year with committing eight murders, is charged with murdering a further seven patients. (→ October 5)

Westminster, 23
In a statement to Parliament, Prime Minister Tony Blair makes it clear that he favours British membership of the European single currency after the next election "if economic conditions are right". Money is to be made available to key government departments to prepare for adoption of the euro. (→ May 27)

United States, 23
The Levi Strauss company announces that it is closing half of its factories in North America because of falling demand for traditional jeans.

Highbury, 23
Arsenal beat Sheffield United 2-1 in their fifth-round rematch. The game was replayed after Arsenal's original victory was agreed to be unfair.

Britain, 24
The Broadcasting Standards Commission says there is too much "inappropriate" sex on television. It cites an ITV series about prostitution, *Vice – The Sex Trade*, as especially offensive.

Oxford, 26
A First Division game between Oxford United and Sunderland is the first competitive football match broadcast on a "pay-per-view" basis by Sky television.

Westminster, 26
The government is criticized in the House of Commons after the names and addresses of informants who helped the police in the Stephen Lawrence case are published in the appendix to the Lawrence inquiry report. Some MPs are incensed that Home Secretary Jack Straw is not present to answer criticism because "a longstanding personal commitment" required him to go abroad. (→ April 8)

Europe, 28
German scientists claim that, as a result of global warming, spring is now arriving in Europe on average six days earlier than it did 30 years ago.

Lebanon, 28
Israel launches air, land, and sea attacks on Hizbollah guerrilla sites in Lebanon after four Israelis, including a brigadier-general, are killed by bombs planted by Hizbollah in the Israeli-controlled "security zone" in south Lebanon. (→ May 17)

London, Wednesday 24. Comic actor Derek Nimmo, who played Reverend Noot in the TV series *All Gas and Gaiters*, died today at the age of 68.

LONDON, MONDAY 22

Leak of report puts Condon on the spot

Metropolitan Police Commissioner Sir Paul Condon is fighting to keep his job after leaked details from the report of the inquiry into the death of black teenager Stephen Lawrence were published yesterday. The report is outspokenly critical of "institutionalized racism" in the Metropolitan Police.

The leaked excerpts first appeared in early editions of the *Sunday Telegraph*. Home Secretary Jack Straw sought an injunction to ban publication of material from the report ahead of its official release on Wednesday. A court granted a ban on further leaks, but allowed the material already published to be repeated by other news media.

Straw claimed that the early leaking of the report was "unfair to the family and to the police officers involved". Today, Lawrence's parents and the police commissioner were invited to the Home Office to read the whole report. Straw has made it clear that he will not be asking Sir Paul to resign. (→ February 24)

FRANCE, TUESDAY 23

Kosovo peace talks end in frustration

Nato leaders are struggling to dispel the impression that they have been humiliated in the Kosovo peace talks at Rambouillet. The talks adjourned today without Serbia agreeing to Nato's primary demand for the deployment of an international peacekeeping force in the Serb-ruled province. US Secretary of State Madeleine Albright had called any agreement lacking that element "a tabletop without legs".

Nato had committed itself to airstrikes against the Serbs if they failed to accept a peace deal that included the troop deployment. But Nato's stance was undermined by the attitude of the Kosovans, who also refused to sign a peace deal. Not satisfied with the degree of autonomy on offer, they were holding out for a referendum on full independence.

With neither side agreeing to Nato-dictated peace terms, it would have been hard to justify airstrikes against Serbia. The talks will resume in three weeks' time. (→ March 10)

AUSTRIA, THURSDAY 25

Avalanches claim 38 lives at devastated Alpine ski resorts

Winter holidaymakers are today being evacuated from ski resorts in the Austrian Alps after a week of blizzards and avalanches that have left at least 38 people dead.

The heaviest snowfalls for 40 years cut off ski resorts from the outside world and created the conditions for avalanches. On Tuesday afternoon, a wall of snow 6 m high and 200 m wide swept down from a ridge above the village of Galtür, destroying everything in its path, including hotels packed with holidaymakers. In atrocious weather conditions, it was 15 hours before outside rescuers reached the scene by helicopter. The following day, another avalanche struck the neighbouring hamlet of Valzur, causing more deaths.

Across the entire Alpine region, it has been one of the worst years for avalanches this century, costing more than 70 lives in total this winter.

The ruins of the village of Galtür, site of Austria's worst avalanche disaster for four decades.

Lawrence report calls for an end to racism

The parents of Stephen Lawrence, in front of an image of their murdered son, at a press conference after the publication of the report: Mrs Lawrence told the press, "Nothing has changed."

The report of the official inquiry into the murder of black teenager Stephen Lawrence in 1993 has made 70 recommendations designed to drive racism out of the police force and other British institutions. Written by Sir William Macpherson, who presided over the inquiry, the report condemns the investigation of the murder as marred by "professional incompetence, institutional racism, and a failure of leadership by senior officers".

Home Secretary Jack Straw, who set up the inquiry, said he hoped the report would be "a catalyst for permanent and irrevocable change" in British society. Prime Minister Tony Blair praised Stephen's parents for the "courage and dignity" with which they had pursued the truth about their son's death, and he called on the British people to find "the will to overcome the racism that still exists within our society".

Metropolitan Police Commissioner Sir Paul Condon said that the police felt "a sense of shame" at the quality of the investigation into the murder. He promised urgent measures to eradicate racism in the police force.

But Doreen Lawrence, Stephen's mother, claimed that nothing had changed since her son's death: "What I see is that black people are still dying in the streets and the back of police vans." Referring to the failure of the police and courts to convict anyone for the murder, she said: "This society has stood by and allowed my son's killers to make a mockery of the law." (→ February 25)

Eltham, Thursday 25. A memorial stone marking the spot where teenager Stephen Lawrence died was today defaced by vandals. Embarrassed police officers admitted that a surveillance camera supposedly monitoring the site was in fact a fake. (→ February 26)

S	M	T	W	T	F	S
	1	2	3	4	5	6
7	8	9	10	11	12	13
14	15	16	17	18	19	20
21	22	23	24	25	26	27
28	29	30	31			

Switzerland, 1
Another attempt to circumnavigate the world by balloon gets off the ground as *Breitling Orbiter 3* takes off from Chateau d'Oex, piloted by Bertrand Piccard and Brian Jones. (→ March 7)

Britain, 1
The Royal Commission on Long-Term Care calls for an extra £1 billion of government money to be spent on looking after the elderly.

London, 2
Accepting the WH Smith Literary Award for her novel *Master Georgie*, Liverpool-born author Beryl Bainbridge derides Scouse accents as "stupid" and calls for elocution lessons in all schools.

London, 2
The FA charges footballers Robbie Fowler and Graham Le Saux with misconduct after last Saturday's match between Chelsea and Liverpool. Fowler allegedly goaded Le Saux with remarks suggesting he was gay. (→ April 9)

Iran, 4
In a severe setback for Islamic hardliners, supporters of Iran's President Khatami, a moderate, triumph in local elections.

Britain, 6
Cathy Woodhead, former wife of Chief Inspector of Schools Chris Woodhead, claims that he had an affair with a pupil when he was a teacher in the 1970s. Mr Woodhead denies the allegation.

North London, 6
Seven people are killed, including three young children, in an arson attack on a house in Chingford.

Paris, 6
In the rugby Five Nations tournament, Wales beat reigning champions France 33-34. It is the Welsh team's first win on French soil since 1975. (→ April 11)

Pacific Ocean, 7
The Cable and Wireless balloon piloted by Colin Prescot and Andy Elson ditches in the sea off Japan, ending their attempt to fly around the world. (→ March 21)

DEATHS
March 5. Lord Denning, controversial judge, dies in Winchester aged 100.

March 7. Stanley Kubrick, American-born British film director whose movies included *Lolita*, *Dr Strangelove*, and *2001: A Space Odyssey*, dies aged 70.

UGANDA, WEDNESDAY 3
Tourists butchered on gorilla safari

Eight tourists on a gorilla-tracking safari in western Uganda have been hacked to death by Hutu rebels. Four of the dead were British. The other victims were from the United States and New Zealand.

The tourists were kidnapped when the rebels attacked a camp in Uganda's Bwindi National Park on Monday. Four Ugandans died resisting the attack. Fourteen tourists, selected by the rebels because they spoke English, were marched towards the Congolese border.

The killings occurred piecemeal in the course of the march. Victims were led away and murdered with machetes and axes. The six survivors were abandoned when the rebels crossed the border into the Congo.

Notes left by the rebels on their victims' bodies blamed Britain and America for supporting the Hutus' traditional enemies, the Tutsi. Hutu death squads massacred 500,000 Tutsi in Rwanda in 1994.

LONDON, FRIDAY 5
Spice baby Brooklyn born

David Beckham and Victoria Adams leave hospital with a well wrapped-up Brooklyn.

Spice Girl Victoria Adams gave birth to a baby boy at the Portland Hospital, London, last night. The baby's father, footballer David Beckham, said it was "the best thing that's ever happened to me". The baby has been named Brooklyn because the couple were in New York when Victoria discovered that she was pregnant.

Little Brooklyn has already earned an estimated £250,000, the sum paid by *OK!* magazine for exclusive post-birth photographs. (→ July 4)

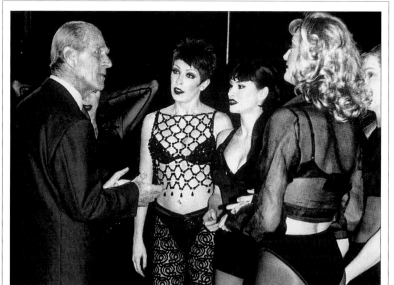

London, Thursday 4. The Queen and the Duke of Edinburgh were given a behind-the-scenes look at London's theatreland today. The Duke (above) met some of the chorus line of *Chicago* at the Adelphi, while the Queen attended a rehearsal of *Oklahoma!* at the Lyceum.

WESTMINSTER, THURSDAY 4
"Banana War" splits Europe and US

West Indian bananas are threatening to cause a transatlantic trade war with serious consequences for businesses in Europe, including Britain.

The United States claims that EU countries discriminate against bananas grown by US companies in Latin America by offering favourable terms to West Indian banana producers.

The Americans yesterday threatened to retaliate by imposing 100 per cent import duties on a range of goods from Europe, including cashmere sweaters and shortbread from Scotland. Britain has protested in the most vigorous terms. Prime Minister Tony Blair described the American action as "unacceptable" and said: "We won't have it." (→ April 9)

Charles reignites beef-on-the-bone controversy with meal of "absolutely delicious" banned meat

Prince Charles sparked a political controversy today when, along with Welsh Secretary Alun Michael, he feasted on a plate of sirloin that had been cooked on the bone. Selling beef on the bone has been illegal since December 1997, when a ban was imposed because of a small risk that the meat might be infected with BSE, the "mad cow" disease.

The Prince of Wales was served the meat at a Welsh food promotion event. He was not actually breaking the law in eating the meat, but it may have been illegal for his hosts to have served it, even though it was a gift.

Alan Duncan, Tory health spokesman, called for the lifting of the ban, claiming that the incident showed how "stupid and idiotic" it was. Prince Charles did not comment on the ban, but declared the meat "absolutely delicious".

Prince Charles accepts a plate of meat that the government has declared a danger to health.

Pop legend Springfield dies of cancer

Dusty Springfield, widely regarded as the best British female vocalist of the 1960s, tonight finally lost a five-year battle against breast cancer. She was 59 years old.

Born Mary O'Brien, she recorded with the Springfields folk group before releasing her first solo hit, "I Only Want to Be with You", in 1963. Her best work was over by 1968, although she made a successful comeback in the 1980s. She received an OBE just four weeks ago at the Royal Marsden Hospital.

Pop idol Dusty Springfield in the 1960s.

Final goodnight for News at Ten

With the words: "So finally, it's good night from *News at Ten*", newsreader Trevor McDonald tonight marked the end of a television era, winding up the last broadcast of a programme that had provided the evening news on ITV for 32 years.

News at Ten is being replaced by news programmes at 6.30 p.m. and 11 p.m. in order to free up ITV's evening schedules. Critics claim that its disappearance is evidence of television "dumbing down". The change was opposed by, among others, Prime Minister Tony Blair, Culture Secretary Chris Smith, and a House of Commons select committee.

Melbourne, Sunday 7. This year's Formula One motor racing season opened today with a surprise victory for Irish driver Eddie Irvine (left) in the Australian Grand Prix. It was Irvine's first grand prix win and he celebrated on the podium with the traditional "champagne bath". (→ April 11)

Port of Spain, Trinidad, 8
In the first Test of their series against Australia, the once-formidable West Indies cricketers are bowled out for 51 in the second innings, their lowest-ever total in a Test match.

Paris, 9
Former French health minister Edmond Hervé is allowed to walk free, despite being found guilty of manslaughter for his part in an HIV-infected blood scandal of the 1980s. Over 4,000 haemophiliacs and hospital patients were infected through the use of unscreened blood, five of them dying of AIDS.

Israel, 9
An Israeli Arab, 21-year-old Rana Raslan, is crowned Miss Israel. It is the first time that an Arab has been selected to represent Israel in the Miss World beauty pageant.

Buenos Aires, 10
Argentinian Vice-President Carlos Ruckauf calls comments made by Prince Charles "intolerable", after the Prince of Wales refers obliquely to Argentina's relations with the people of the Falklands in a speech made at a state dinner. Prince Charles is in Argentina on what is supposed to be a bridge-building visit.

Kosovo, 10
More than 4,000 Kosovan refugees are displaced as Serb forces mount a co-ordinated attack on five ethnic Albanian villages near the Macedonian border. Yugoslav President Slobodan Milosevic continues to oppose the deployment of a Nato peacekeeping force in Kosovo. (→ March 14)

Wembley, 11
Wembley Stadium is sold for £103 million to a group backed by the Football Association. The consortium plans to demolish the 76-year-old stadium next year and, with an eye on the 2006 World Cup, replace it with a 90,000-seat stadium by August 2003.

DEATHS
March 8. Joe DiMaggio, star baseball centrefielder for the Yankees during the 1930s and 1940s, and briefly married to actress Marilyn Monroe in 1954, dies of lung cancer, aged 84.

March 10. Adrian Love, radio DJ for more than 30 years, dies following a second lung collapse, aged 54.

BELFAST, THURSDAY 11
Clegg cleared of murder charge

In the final twist to a nine-year legal saga, paratrooper Lance Corporal Lee Clegg was today acquitted of the murder of joyrider Karen Reilly.

In September 1990 Clegg's patrol fired on a stolen car at a checkpoint in west Belfast, killing the driver and 18-year-old Ms Reilly, who was in the back seat. Convicted of her murder in 1993, Clegg was released from prison on licence in 1995 after a public outcry in Britain. His release, however, sparked widespread rioting in nationalist areas of Ulster. A retrial was ordered last year.

Retrial judge Justice Kerr said today that Clegg had invented a "farrago of untruths" to save his skin, but that it was impossible to be sure that he had fired the fatal shot. The judge found him guilty on a second charge of attempting to wound the driver, but legal experts believe Clegg is unlikely to be sent back to prison.

YORKSHIRE, TUESDAY 9
Floods sweep the Derwent Valley

Towns and villages along the River Derwent are facing their worst floods this century. The river has been swollen by heavy rain and melting snow on the moors. In the market town of Malton and nearby Norton more than 100 families have had to flee their homes. Local Tory MP John Greenway said it was "the worst disaster in most people's memory".

Paris, Wednesday 10. British design talent stole the limelight at the Paris fashion shows today. Among Stella McCartney's collection for Chloë were sexy evening dresses with attitude (left) and rock-chic denims, while **Alexander McQueen presented a futuristic look for Givenchy, including bodymoulding and high-neck bodysuits made of electrical circuitry print material (right).**

WESTMINSTER, TUESDAY 9

Brown delivers up-beat budget

A cheerful, confident chancellor on his way to announce tax cuts and spending growth.

Chancellor of the Exchequer Gordon Brown drew cheers from Labour benches today with an unexpected promise to cut the basic rate of income tax from 23p to 22p in the pound, and the introduction of a 10p tax band for low earners. He also announced more money for families with children and for pensioners.

In a budget dedicated to "enterprise and fairness", the chancellor promised a higher standard of living "not for the few, but for all of us".

Taxes on tobacco and petrol will rise, however, and mortgage tax relief is to be abolished. Tory leader William Hague denounced Brown as "a pickpocket chancellor" raising taxes by stealth. (→ March 22)

Berlin, Friday 12. Violinist Lord Yehudi Menuhin died today, aged 82. A child prodigy, he first performed in public at the age of seven. In his later years he was noted for his charitable work.

BERLIN, THURSDAY 11

Red Oskar out in German political storm

Germany's powerful finance minister, Oskar Lafontaine, resigned today after a row with the leader of the country's Social Democrat government, Chancellor Gerhard Schröder. Named "the most dangerous man in Europe" by the *Sun* newspaper because of his enthusiasm for greater European integration, Lafontaine had scared German business leaders with his old-style socialist policies.

WESTMINSTER, MONDAY 8

Right-to-roam joy for ramblers

The government today outlined new legislation that will give ramblers the legal right of access to four million acres of mountains and moorland. Michael Meacher, the environment minister, said that land currently "the preserve of the few" would be open "for the delight of the many".

The Ramblers' Association hailed victory in "a century-long struggle". But the representatives of large landowners reacted angrily, accusing the government of "destroying the goodwill of the countryside".

NEW YORK, SATURDAY 13

Title fight ends in uproar as Lewis is denied crown

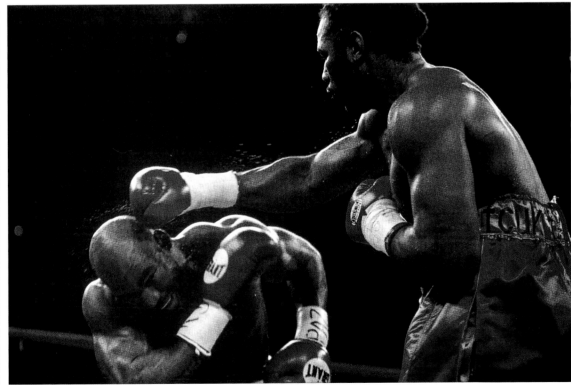

Lennox Lewis lands yet another blow on Evander Holyfield's head – such punches were apparently invisible to two of the ringside judges.

Two ringside judges in Madison Square Garden tonight denied British heavyweight Lennox Lewis the chance to become undisputed world champion, after a bout in which he appeared to have trounced American boxer Evander Holyfield.

Lewis raised his fist in triumph at the end of the fight, only to learn that the judges had given a split decision. One judge declared Lewis the winner, but Briton Larry O'Connel called it even, and American Jean Williams gave it to Holyfield.

The verdict was greeted with boos and gasps of disbelief. According to an unofficial count, Lewis landed 348 punches to Holyfield's 130. Roy Jones, of the American cable network HBO, said the decision made him "ashamed to be an American".

S	M	T	W	T	F	S
	1	2	3	4	5	6
7	8	9	10	11	12	13
14	15	16	17	18	19	20
21	22	23	24	25	26	27
28	29	30	31			

Kosovo, 14

As Serb and ethnić Albanian delegations arrive in Paris to resume talks on Kosovo, Serb soldiers launch attacks on several Kosovan villages. (→ March 21)

Turkey, 15

Kurdish militants urge tourists to avoid Turkey's Mediterranean resorts as they mount a bombing campaign in response to the arrest of their leader Abdullah Ocalan last month. Fourteen people have been killed by bombs in the last three days in Ankara and Istanbul. (→ May 31)

Strasbourg, 15

The European Commission on Human Rights rules that the two boys who murdered two-year-old James Bulger in 1993 should not have been tried in an adult Crown Court.

New York, 16

Traders on Wall Street celebrate as the Dow Jones index passes the 10,000 mark for the first time. It has risen 6,000 points in four and a half years.

Lord's, 16

The first ten women members of the MCC enter the Long Room at Lord's cricket ground. The club voted last year to admit women to its ranks.

London, 16

The Office for National Statistics reveals that half of all pregnancies in England and Wales now occur outside marriage.

Milan, 17

Manchester United draw 1-1 with Inter Milan, beating Inter 3-1 on aggregate and securing a place in the European Cup semifinals. (→ April 21)

London, 19

The Economist publishes a report claiming that Rupert Murdoch's Newscorp has avoided paying corporation tax in the UK for the past 11 years despite making a profit in the UK of £1.387 billion.

Belfast, 19

Four IRA killers are convicted of murder, but will serve only 16 months of their sentence under the terms of the Good Friday agreement. (→ April 1)

DEATHS

March 17. Rod Hull, entertainer and creator of the belligerent Emu puppet, dies in a fall from a roof, aged 63.

March 20. Patrick Heron, CBE, painter and art critic, dies aged 79.

Hollywood, Sunday 21. At the Academy Awards this evening British movie *Shakespeare in Love* won seven Oscars, including the award for best picture. Gwyneth Paltrow (left), who won best leading actress for her part in the film, sobbed as she made a highly emotional acceptance speech. A more composed Judi Dench (above) was voted best supporting actress for her role as Elizabeth I. Steven Spielberg's World War II epic *Saving Private Ryan* had been widely tipped to win the best picture award, but Spielberg had to be content with best director. Roberto Benigni's touching comedy *Life Is Beautiful* won best foreign film.

N. IRELAND, MONDAY 15
Loyalist bomb kills rights lawyer Rosemary Nelson

Lawyer Rosemary Nelson, a prominent defender of the rights of Catholics in Northern Ireland, died today when a bomb blew up her car near her home in Lurgan, County Armagh. A loyalist terrorist group, the Red Hand Defenders, said it was responsible. The killing is a major setback for efforts to revive the flagging Ulster peace process. (→ March 19)

BRUSSELS, TUESDAY 16
European Commissioners quit in corruption scandal

The European Union was plunged into political crisis last night when the entire European Commission resigned in response to the damning conclusions of an inquiry into mismanagement, fraud, and nepotism in the Brussels bureaucracy.

The inquiry was set up in January to pacify the European parliament, which was threatening a vote of no confidence in the Commission. Few expected the inquiry's conclusions to be so devastating. The report spoke of "a loss of control by the political authorities over the administration that they are supposedly running". It was especially critical of the French Commissioner Edith Cresson.

Despite resigning, the Commission president, Jacques Santer, claimed that the report was "distorted". But European leaders made it clear today that Santer would be replaced as soon as possible. (→ March 24)

Nato on brink of air war

Nato leaders today threatened Serb leader Slobodan Milosevic with airstrikes "within a few hours" if he continued to reject a peace deal that would put a Nato-led peacekeeping force into the province of Kosovo.

Six days ago, representatives of the ethnic Albanian majority in Kosovo accepted a Nato proposal that would give the province limited self-rule. This allowed Nato to turn the heat on the Serbs, now seen as the only obstacle on the road to peace.

Even as talks went on in Paris last week, Serbia was mounting an offensive against Kosovan guerrillas, and growing numbers of Kosovan refugees were fleeing their homes in the face of Serb terror. President Bill Clinton used reports of massacres to justify the threat of airstrikes. He told Americans that there should not be "thousands more people slaughtered … before we do something."

Today, Nato aircraft and warships armed with cruise missiles are in position to attack Serbia. Unarmed peace monitors have been withdrawn from Kosovo. Foreign Secretary Robin Cook said that Milosevic was leaving Nato leaders "no option but military action". (→ March 24)

Round-the-world balloon flight triumph at last

Balloonist Brian Jones celebrates the end of his historic journey.

After repeated failed attempts by high-profile personalities, such as Virgin boss Richard Branson and American millionaire Steve Fossett, the feat of flying a balloon nonstop around the world has been achieved at last by a pair of relative unknowns, Bertrand Piccard from Switzerland and Brian Jones from Britain.

At dawn this morning, the *Breitling Orbiter 3* bounced down to earth in a remote desert spot about 500 miles from Cairo. The two balloonists had spent exactly three weeks in the air.

They completed the circumnavigation of the globe just before 10 a.m. GMT yesterday, when their balloon passed 9 degrees longitude above Mauritania, northwest Africa. The two balloonists celebrated their victorious 29,000-mile journey with a cup of tea.

When they touched down this morning their morale was high even though there was no audience of supporters to greet them. Various teams of reporters and technical experts attempted to reach the balloonists, but all foundered because of either the terrain or Egyptian red tape. It was not until eight hours later that a military helicopter finally picked them out of the desert.

According to Piccard, while they waited to be rescued from the desert they "spent a few hours looking at the sand, sun, the sky. Very calm."

Race to be London's mayor hots up

Ken Livingstone (left) and Jeffrey Archer, political mavericks hoping to be mayor.

A third man today joined the race to become London's first directly elected mayor. Broadcaster Trevor Phillips, presenter of LWT's *London Programme* and a friend of former minister Peter Mandelson, wants to be Labour's candidate for the post.

Labour MP and former head of the GLC Ken Livingstone and bestselling novelist and former Tory MP Lord Archer of Weston-super-Mare have already put themselves forward. Both will have a struggle to be adopted by their parties as a candidate, however. Lord Archer has a chequered past and Livingstone has often been at odds with the current Labour leadership. (→ October 1)

Slough, Sunday 21. Comedian Ernie Wise, aged 73, died in hospital today of heart failure. With the late Eric Morecombe, he created a comic double act that reached its creative peak in popular TV shows of the 1970s.

S	M	T	W	T	F	S
	1	2	3	4	5	6
7	8	9	10	11	12	13
14	15	16	17	18	19	20
21	22	23	24	25	26	27
28	29	30	31			

London, 22
Truckers protesting at road tax and diesel fuel tax increases block Park Lane with over 700 lorries for an hour, causing traffic chaos in central London.

Serbia, 24
Eighty Nato warplanes and about 100 cruise missiles batter targets in Serbia. It is Nato's first offensive against a sovereign state in its 50-year history. (→ March 29)

London, 24
The BBC announces that Ross Kemp, alias Grant Mitchell in *EastEnders*, will leave the programme in August. The star has clinched a £1 million deal with ITV.

Brussels, 24
Former Italian prime minister Romano Prodi is chosen as the new president of the European Commission. (→ July 9)

United States, 25
Thirteen-year-old Welsh singer Charlotte Church becomes the youngest soloist ever to enter the US Top 30 album charts with *Voice of an Angel*.

Edinburgh, 25
Mohammed Sarwar, suspended Labour MP for Glasgow Govan, is acquitted of bribery and vote-rigging allegations after a 40-day trial at the High Court in Edinburgh. He will now be reinstated.

London, 25
Robbie Williams, former member of the band Take That, loses his acrimonious legal battle with former manager Nigel Martin-Smith. He must now pay Martin-Smith £90,000 in royalty fees.

London, 26
Chelsea coach Graham Rix is sentenced to a year in prison for having unlawful sex with a 15-year-old girl.

Pontiac, Michigan, 26
Euthanasia campaigner Dr Jack Kevorkian, dubbed "Doctor Death" after helping more than 130 people to commit suicide, is convicted of the murder of Thomas Youk. He videoed himself giving Youk a lethal injection. (→ April 13).

Wembley, 27
Paul Scholes scores a hat trick as England beat Poland 3-1 in Kevin Keegan's first match as England manager. (→ April 28)

Ukraine, 31
Anatoli Onoprienko, nicknamed "the Terminator", is found guilty of 52 murders, making him possibly the most practised and notorious serial killer ever.

Mont Blanc, Sunday 28. Firefighters today found the wreckage of 25 lorries and nine cars in the Mont Blanc tunnel after a blaze that raged there last week. At least 40 people were killed in the fire, which apparently started when a Belgian lorry caught fire.

Pinochet case stumbles forward

Anti-Pinochet protesters comment on the general's close relationship with Baroness Thatcher.

In a judgement that created much confusion, the Law Lords today ruled that General Augusto Pinochet could be extradited to Spain, but only for torture offenses committed after September 1988, when Britain signed the UN Torture Convention.

The ruling means that only three of the 30 charges against Pinochet stand, and Pinochet supporters have called on Home Secretary Jack Straw to halt extradition. But he seems likely to repeat his earlier authorization to proceed. (→ April 15)

Refugees flee

Five days ago, Nato began airstrikes against targets in Serbia, intending to end the Serb policy of "ethnic cleansing" in the rebel province of Kosovo and impose a peace agreement giving the Kosovans a large measure of self-government. But Serb leader Slobodan Milosevic has responded with defiance, ordering a major offensive in Kosovo to drive out the ethnic Albanian population and crush the guerrillas of the Kosovo Liberation Army (KLA).

Today the region is facing a colossal refugee crisis as an estimated 150,000 ethnic Albanians flee the Serb security forces, heading for neighbouring Macedonia and Albania. Many refugees have been ordered from their towns and villages at gun point. Often, young men have been led away by Serb forces to an uncertain fate, separated from their

as Nato air onslaught fails to curb Serb terror drive

Kosovan refugees leave their homes for exile. Most are old men, women, and children — men of fighting age were taken away by the Serbs.

out a land invasion of Kosovo since they are convinced that popular sentiment in their countries is not ready to accept the heavy casualties that a ground war would entail. British Foreign Secretary Robin Cook said today that there was "no intention and no plan to commit ground troops". The Serbs are believed to have around 27,000 soldiers, more than 16,000 police special forces, and about 300 tanks inside Kosovo.

Both US President Bill Clinton and British Prime Minister Tony Blair today reaffirmed their commitment to the military conflict. Blair promised that he would "see it through to a successful conclusion" and warned Milosevic that he would pay a "higher and higher price" for the continuing atrocities in Kosovo.

Britain has named Milosevic among a number of key figures in the Serb government, army, and security forces who could face prosecution for war crimes after the conflict ends. (→ April 3)

Serbia, Sunday 28. Serb villagers today danced on the wing of a US Stealth bomber shot down outside Belgrade. Captain Ken Dwelle, the pilot, was snatched to safety by an American combat rescue team.

A cruise missile is fired from a warship in the Adriatic against a target in Serbia.

families who were driven out onto the roads. Other refugees have simply fled in terror as the fighting drew near to their homes.

UN officials attempting to cope with the massive influx of refugees into Macedonia today spoke of an impending "humanitarian catastrophe" if the international community failed to respond quickly to the need for food, medicines, and shelter.

Nato leaders are struggling to respond to a situation that has developed in a wholly unexpected way. Airstrikes have been followed by a massive escalation in the ethnic cleansing they were intended to stop.

Nato has overwhelming destructive power at its disposal, with 400 aircraft and an unspecified number of cruise missiles now available for

the conflict. A Nato spokesman claimed today that "colossal damage" had been inflicted on the infrastructure of the Serb army and police. The air campaign had begun with the destruction of Serbia's air defence systems, followed by attacks on arms factories located near the Serb capital, Belgrade. Nato also successfully targeted ministry of defence and police buildings in Kosovo's main city, Pristina. Now Nato intends to turn its air power against Serb troops in Kosovo.

But Nato airstrikes have been inhibited by a desire to avoid civilian casualties, and they have also been hampered by bad weather. The air campaign has clearly failed so far to halt the Serb campaign of terror. Nato leaders have, however, ruled

Northern Ireland, 1
The British and Irish governments issue the Hillsborough Declaration, which aims to set up an Ulster executive following the handover of arms. But Sinn Fein is unhappy with the deal. (→ April 13)

Birmingham, 4
Britain's tennis players are beaten 3-2 by the US in the first round of the Davis Cup, after Greg Rusedski loses the final match to Jim Courier in five sets.

Utrecht, 5
Following a deal made between Libyan leader Colonel Gadaffi and the UN, the two Libyans suspected of the 1988 Lockerbie bombing arrive in the Netherlands, where they will be tried before three Scottish judges.

East Timor, 6
At least 40 people die when Indonesian-backed paramilitaries storm a church at Liquica that was sheltering 2,000 East Timorese. East Timor is seeking independence from Indonesia.

Belgrade, 6
Serbia offers Nato a ceasefire. Serb troops in Kosovo would return to barracks and refugees would be allowed back to their homes. The offer is rejected by Nato as a cynical ploy. (→ April 7)

Old Bailey, 7
Edgar Pearce, 61, admits to being the "Mardi Gra bomber". Between 1994 and 1998, he planted 36 bombs across London and the Home Counties in an attempt to extort money from Barclays Bank and Sainsbury's. (→ April 14)

London, 8
ITV broadcasts an interview with the five chief suspects in the Stephen Lawrence murder case. The interview is denounced by Stephen's father, Neville Lawrence, as a "publicity stunt". (→ April 21)

Andover, 9
Mary Chipperfield is fined £7,500 for ill treatment of a chimpanzee in her care. But no order is made to prevent her from working with animals in the future.

Moscow, 9
President Boris Yeltsin warns Nato "not to push Russia towards military action" over Kosovo. (→ April 12)

Washington, D.C., 9
The US government removes British exports, including shortbread and cashmere, from its "Banana War" hit list.

BELGRADE, THURSDAY 1

Abducted US soldiers "to be tried"

Three battered US soldiers, Ramirez, Stone, and Gonzales, are paraded on Serb television.

Three American soldiers, members of a cavalry scout reconnaissance unit, have been snatched by Serb forces and exhibited on state television. According to reports from Nato headquarters, the three captured soldiers, staff sergeants Andrew Ramirez and Christopher Stone and Specialist Steven Gonzales, were operating inside the Former Yugoslav Republic of Macedonia when Serb troops ambushed them, then carried them across the border into Kosovo. Serbia today said that it intended to put the soldiers on trial for espionage. If found guilty, they could face 20 years in a Serbian prison.

The men looked battered and dazed as they lined up for the TV cameras. Their haggard appearance caused a sense of shock in the United States. President Bill Clinton issued a grave warning to the Serb leader, Slobodan Milosevic, saying: "President Milosevic should make no mistake, the United States takes care of its own. We will hold him and his government responsible for their safety and for their well-being."

The public humiliation of the three soldiers and their apparent mistreatment has at last brought home to the American people the fact that their country is at war. (→ May 2)

BELGRADE, SATURDAY 3

Belgrade burns in Nato blitz

Nato's air war against Serbia took on a new ferocity last night as buildings in the centre of the Serb capital, Belgrade, were hit by a salvo of eight cruise missiles. The twin Serb and Yugoslav interior ministry buildings exploded in a huge fireball.

The onslaught reflected a new "no-holds-barred" policy agreed by Nato political leaders yesterday. Since the air attacks have so far failed to shake Serb resistance, Nato has decided to escalate the conflict.

There were no reports of deaths in the attack – the ministry buildings had been evacuated days ago. But the explosions caused panic in a medical centre close by, packed with mothers and newborn children.

Angry Serbs compared the attack to the bombing of the city by the Germans in 1941. Deputy Prime Minister Vuk Draskovic called it "a crime against the Serb nation and the charter of the UN". (→ April 6)

Serb firemen struggle to contain a blaze caused by one of Nato's Tomahawk missiles.

Aintree, Saturday 10. Bobbyjo, ridden by Paul Carberry, streamed into the lead after the final fence to win the Grand National in style today. It was the first Irish victory since Paul's father and Bobbyjo's trainer, Tommy Carberry, won with L'Escargot 24 years ago.

Fowler sniff earns record fine

At an FA disciplinary hearing in Birmingham today, Liverpool and England footballer Robbie Fowler was fined £32,000 and banned for six games after two misplaced "jokes" on the football field.

In a match against Chelsea last month, Fowler allegedly taunted his England colleague Graham Le Saux with being a homosexual, at one point wiggling his bottom suggestively. Then, last Saturday, after scoring against Liverpool's Merseyside rivals, Everton, he knelt down and pretended to snort cocaine from a white line on the pitch.

Fowler admitted that his actions had been "stupid". He has agreed to help in an anti-drugs campaign.

Fowler celebrates a goal by sniffing a line.

Kosovan refugee crisis mounts

The former refugee camp at Blace, Macedonia, littered with abandoned belongings after Macedonian troops drove out the Kosovans.

The action of the Macedonian authorities in clearing nearly 30,000 Kosovan refugees from a crowded camp at Blace in the middle of the night has been condemned by the United Nations High Commission for Refugees (UNHCR) today. Most were not given time to assemble their possessions before being herded onto buses and driven off. The majority were taken across the border into neighbouring Albania.

The Macedonians' brusque action has again highlighted the refugees' difficult predicament. Some 400,000 Kosovans have now taken refuge in Macedonia and Albania, a massive burden for two small countries to bear. So far international relief efforts have failed to cope with the scale of the crisis. Nato leaders are committed to airlifting refugees out of the war zone, but not in the numbers or time required. (→ April 9)

Murdoch bid for United blocked

The government today announced that it was blocking a bid by BSkyB to take over Manchester United Football Club. The decision followed an adverse report by the Monopolies and Mergers Commission.

The decision is a victory for Manchester fans, who campaigned hard against the takeover, and a rebuff for BSkyB's owner, Rupert Murdoch. A BSkyB executive said "emotion had won out over facts."

Guilty verdict in Britain's first war crimes trial

Anthony Sawoniuk, a 78-year-old former British Rail employee, today became the only person ever to be convicted by a British court of Nazi war crimes. He was sentenced to two terms of life imprisonment for the murder of 18 Jews in his native Belarus during World War II.

Recruited by the Germans in 1941, Sawoniuk led "search and kill" missions against Jews, probably causing many more deaths than those with which he was charged. He has lived in Britain since 1947.

S	M	T	W	T	F	S
				1	2	3
4	5	6	7	8	9	10
11	12	13	14	15	16	17
18	19	20	21	22	23	24
25	26	27	28	29	30	

São Paulo, 11
Mika Hakkinen wins the Brazilian Grand Prix, five seconds ahead of his nearest rival, Michael Schumacher. (→ May 2)

Pontiac, Michigan, 13
Dr Jack Kevorkian, 70-year-old euthanasia campaigner, is sentenced to 10-25 years in prison for murder after he carries out an "assisted suicide".

Westminster, 13
For the second time within a year, the House of Lords rejects a bill, passed by the House of Commons, to lower the age of consent for gay sex from 18 to 16.

Pakistan, 14
Three days after India tests a long-range missile capable of carrying a nuclear warhead, Pakistan responds with its own long-range missile test. (→ May 28)

Westminster, 14
In response to the recommendations of the Lawrence inquiry, Home Secretary Jack Straw orders police in England and Wales to recruit more than 8,000 black and Asian officers over the next ten years.

Old Bailey, 14
Edgar Pearce, the "Mardi Gra bomber", is sentenced to 21 years in prison, despite evidence that he is suffering from a degenerative brain condition.

Birmingham, 14
Carla Germaine and Greg Cordell, who had never met before marrying 11 weeks ago as part of a radio contest, announce that their marriage is over.

Villa Park, 14
Manchester United's Ryan Giggs scores a memorable goal against Arsenal in extra time to send his team to the FA Cup final. Arsenal's boss Arsene Wenger describes his team's 2-1 semifinal defeat as "unlucky". (→ May 22)

Kosovo, 15
Nato admits "mistakenly" bombing a convoy of ethnic Albanian refugees. Many refugees were reportedly killed in the incident. (→ April 17)

Westminster, 15
Home Secretary Jack Straw gives the go-ahead for extradition proceedings against General Pinochet. (→ October 8)

Massachusetts, 15
Astronomers at the Harvard-Smithsonian Institute announce the discovery of the first known planetary system beyond our own. It lies 44 light years away.

Jose Maria Olazabal dons the coveted Green Jacket after his triumph at Augusta National.

Masterly return for Spanish ace Olazabal

Spanish golfer Jose Maria Olazabal held his nerve through the last round of the US Masters today to take his second Masters trophy by two strokes from American Davis Love III. It was a remarkable personal comeback for the 33-year-old Spaniard, who was forced out of golf in 1995 by a crippling back ailment. Since returning to the game in 1997 he had struggled to recover his form.

NORTHERN IRELAND, TUESDAY 13

Irish peace process stalled over arms decommissioning

Efforts to install a power-sharing executive in Northern Ireland, in fulfilment of last year's Good Friday Agreement, were stalemated today as Sinn Fein rejected an Anglo-Irish initiative requiring the IRA and other paramilitary groups to begin decommissioning arms. Known as the Hillsborough Declaration, the initiative was drawn up by the British and Irish governments two weeks ago. It calls for the establishment of a power-sharing executive, including Sinn Fein, to be followed a month later by "a collective act of conciliation", in which loyalist and republican paramilitaries would make a move towards disarmament. Ulster Unionists are refusing to sit in an executive with Sinn Fein unless the IRA begins to disarm. (→ June 5)

LONDON, SATURDAY 17

Police hunt for Brixton bomber

Police are today searching for a "disturbed" individual who left a bomb in a black holdall in a crowded south London market.

The bomb, packed with nails, exploded at 5.26 p.m. in the centre of Brixton as Saturday shopping was at its peak. No warning was given. About 50 people were injured, some of them seriously – a 23-month-old boy had a nail buried in his head.

The bomb was described by police as a crude homemade device. Any involvement of Irish terrorist groups was quickly ruled out. Brixton has a large West Indian community, and some local residents suggested that a racist organization may have been responsible.

Police have begun studying film from security cameras around the market in the hope of identifying the bomber. (→ April 24)

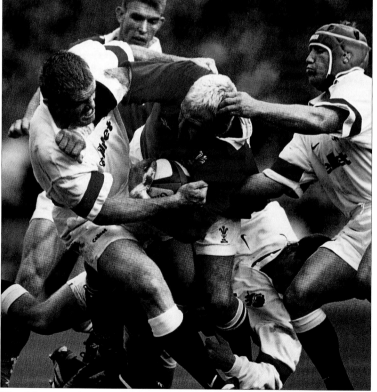

Wembley, Sunday 11. In a sensational end to the rugby Five Nations Championship today, Wales beat England 31-32 with an injury-time try by Scott Gibbs from a pass by Scott Quinnell (centre above). The Welsh victory allowed Scotland to win the championship.

KOSOVO, MONDAY 12

Support for war wavers as Nato hits civilians

The wreckage at Yezhna Morava River of the passenger train that was hit by two Nato missiles, killing ten civilians.

Anti-Nato protests took place both in Serbia and in Nato countries.

Nato sources confirmed tonight that a warplane targeting a railway bridge in southeast Serbia had inadvertently hit a passenger train, killing ten people and injuring another 16.

The Nato statement came after the Serb authorities bused foreign journalists to the site, a bridge over the Yezhna Morava River. One missile had sliced the train in two as it crossed the bridge, while another smashed into the front carriage. Nine of the dead were incinerated inside the train, while one body was retrieved from the river below.

A Nato official said: "There was no intent to hit the train and we deeply regret any loss of life." But the impact of the incident on public opinion is worrying for Nato. So far protests against the war have been a minority affair, but observers believe that support for the war could evaporate as casualties mount.

Faced with rising doubts, however, Prime Minister Tony Blair yesterday reaffirmed his idealistic view of the war. Writing in *Newsweek*, he said: "We are fighting not for territory but for values, for a new internationalism where the brutal repression of whole ethnic groups will no longer be tolerated." (→ April 15)

KOSOVO, SATURDAY 17

Evidence of massacres by Serb ethnic cleansers

Nato fought back in the intensifying propaganda war with Serbia today by publishing air reconnaissance photographs that seem to show a fresh mass burial site near the Kosovan village of Izbica.

A Nato spokesman said that there was mounting evidence of "a concerted and organized campaign of murder and barbarism" being carried out by Serb forces in Kosovo. Eyewitness accounts from Kosovan refugees have painted a horrific picture of Serb atrocities. (→ April 22)

Two aerials photos of the same area. The more recent one (right) "shows a graveyard".

S	M	T	W	T	F	S
				1	2	3
4	5	6	7	8	9	10
11	12	13	14	15	16	17
18	19	20	21	22	23	24
25	26	27	28	29	30	

Britain, 18
Tracie Andrews, convicted of the murder of her fiancé Lee Harvey last year, admits in a letter to the *News of the World* that she did carry out the killing. At the time of her trial, Andrews insisted she was innocent, claiming Harvey was the victim of a "road rage" attack.

New York, 18
Wayne Gretzky, widely regarded as the greatest ice-hockey player ever, retires after 21 years in the sport.

Berlin, 19
Moving from its previous seat in Bonn, the German parliament meets for the first time in the newly restored Berlin Reichstag building.

Washington, D.C., 20
An IMF (International Monetary Fund) report says that the world economic crisis that began in Asia and Russia in 1997 has passed the worst. The report also states that global economic conditions will continue to improve into the year 2000.

Germany, 21
At an international conference in Bremen, the European Space Agency says that it may soon be possible for tourists to take trips into space, staying at luxury hotels in orbit around the Earth.

London, 21
The parents of murdered teenager Stephen Lawrence begin civil action against the five prime suspects in the case and the Metropolitan Police. (→ July 13)

Belgrade, 22
A Nato missile destroys the headquarters of the Serb state television service, killing at least ten civilians, including journalists, and injuring many more. (→ April 24)

Ontario, 22
Scientists at the University of Western Ontario dispute the findings of US researchers who claimed to have identified a "gay gene". The Canadian scientists say their research concludes that the gene is not linked to homosexuality.

South Africa, 23
Makhaya Ntini, the first black cricketer to play for South Africa and a role model for many young black sportsmen, is found guilty of rape.

Manchester, 23
Bus driver Darren Vickers is sentenced to life imprisonment for the murder of eight-year-old Jamie Lavis in 1997.

LONDON, SATURDAY 24

Mystery bomber strikes again

The aftermath of the Brick Lane bomb: the device exploded in the boot of a maroon Sierra, leaving the car a twisted wreck.

For the second successive Saturday, London has been hit by a bomb attack delivered without warning and clearly intended to kill or maim.

Last week's explosion was in Brixton, with its West Indian community. Today it was the turn of Brick Lane in the East End, home to a large Bangladeshi population.

Deputy Assistant Commissioner Alan Fry, head of Scotland Yard's antiterrorist squad, said this evening that the police were treating the bombings as a racist offence. A right-wing extremist group called Combat 18 phoned to claim responsibility for the bombing. Combat 18 earlier said it carried out the Brixton attack.

No one was killed in the Brick Lane explosion. A passer-by picked up the bomb, which had been left in a bag in the street, and put it in the boot of his car while he tried to contact the police. The bomb went off, destroying the car and hurling nails down the street. Luckily, only six people were slightly injured. (→ April 30)

WESTMINSTER, TUESDAY 20

Call for end to Thatcherism stirs Tory storm

Conservatives were today celebrating the start of Margaret Thatcher's premiership in 1979, which ushered in 18 years of Tory rule. But the occasion coincided with a lecture by deputy leader, Peter Lilley, declaring it was time for the Tories to turn their back on some of the central tenets of Thatcherism. He called for a commitment to publicly funded health care and education, and recognition "that there is more to life … than defending and extending the free market". His speech was condemned by many Tory MPs and shadow ministers. (→ June 15)

Turin, Wednesday 21. Manchester United qualified for the final of the European Cup this evening, beating Juventus 2-3. United were two down within the first ten minutes, but fought back with goals by Keane, Yorke, and Cole (above centre). (→ May 26)

WASHINGTON, D.C., SAT. 24

Nato's birthday under the shadow of war

Nato was founded 50 years ago this month, and leaders of the allied countries were invited to a celebration in Washington, D.C. But the intended birthday party has turned out to be a grim military summit, as Nato struggles to decide what to do next in a war in Kosovo that seems increasingly hard to win.

British Prime Minister Tony Blair, described by one American journalist as "the alliance's most outspoken hawk", is urging preparations for a ground invasion of Kosovo if the air war, now in its fourth week, fails to

Kosovan refugees arrive in Britain as an end to the war remains a distant prospect.

make Serbia back down. But other Nato leaders are either lukewarm about this option or flatly opposed.

Meanwhile, the airlift of Kosovan refugees to Nato countries, begun on Sunday, is well under way. Britain has agreed to take 10,000 refugees. Nato leaders admit that, even if the war is won, a huge aid effort will be needed to resettle the Kosovans and restore regional stability. (→ April 28)

COLORADO, WEDNESDAY 21

School massacre stuns America

Shocked students huddle together for emotional comfort outside Columbine High School.

Littleton, a quiet suburb of Denver, Colorado, was yesterday the scene of carnage as two teenagers ran amok in Columbine High School, killing 12 students and a teacher before turning their guns on themselves.

The attack began shortly after 11 a.m. Dressed in black trenchcoats, Dylan Klebold, 17, and Eric Harris, 18, strode into the school carrying firearms and a store of homemade bombs. Many of their victims were shot at random, but the killers specially selected "jocks" – athletes – as victims, along with blacks and members of other ethnic minorities. Before killing themselves, they left booby-trap bombs around the buildings of the high school .

A profile of the two killers has emerged as poseurs who suffered ridicule at school. They had formed a group called the Trenchcoat Mafia. Obsessed with the Nazis, they timed the massacre to coincide with Hitler's birthday. The FBI is investigating possible links with various right-wing extremist organizations.

President Bill Clinton spoke for most Americans when he said: "All of us are struggling to understand exactly what happened and why." The massacre is bound to rekindle the acrimonious debate about gun control in the US. (→ April 27)

KINGSTON, THURSDAY 22

Jamaicans riot against fuel tax increase

At least nine people have been killed in the worst unrest seen on the Caribbean island of Jamaica for two decades. Rioting broke out on Monday after the government of Percival Patterson announced a steep rise in petrol tax. The government says that tax rises are needed to cope with the country's debt crisis.

In poor districts of the capital, Kingston, protesters blocked streets with hijacked cars and burning tyres, and exchanged fire with security forces. There was widespread looting and arson. The government says it is reconsidering the increase in taxes.

London, Sunday 18. At this year's London Marathon, Mike Gambrill and Barbara Cole interrupted their run to be married by a registrar in Greenwich. The men's race was won by Moroccan Abdelkader El Mouaziz, while Kenyan Joyce Chepchumba won the women's race.

S	M	T	W	T	F	S
				1	2	3
4	5	6	7	8	9	10
11	12	13	14	15	16	17
18	19	20	21	22	23	24
25	26	27	28	29	30	

Rotterdam, 25
Dutch police fire on rioting supporters of Feyenoord Football Club, wounding four people, one critically.

England, 26
Tottenham's winger, Frenchman David Ginola, is voted Professional Footballers' Association Player of the Year.

Maidstone, 27
Two students at a college in Kent, Graham Wallis and Neil Sayers, are convicted of murdering fellow student Russell Crookes in May of last year because "he got on their nerves".

Washington, D.C., 27
In the wake of the Denver school massacre, President Bill Clinton proposes to ban the sale of handguns to people under 21 years old and to make parents potentially responsible for the misuse of firearms by their children.

England, 28
England caretaker football manager Kevin Keegan tells the press he is ready to take on the job permanently.

Belgrade, 28
Vuk Draskovic, Yugoslav deputy prime minister, is sacked by President Slobodan Milosevic after stating publicly that Nato cannot be beaten. (→ April 29)

Geneva, 29
The UN Commission on Human Rights approves a call for a worldwide ban on executions, but nine countries, including China and the United States, abstain.

Belgrade, 29
Russian envoy Viktor Chernomyrdin meets with President Milosevic. Nato is backing Russian efforts to broker a peace deal to end the Kosovo War. (→ May 1)

Westminster, 30
The court of appeal clears former head of Westminster council, Dame Shirley Porter, of misconduct in the "homes for votes" scandal. She had previously been ordered to pay £27 million in surcharges for manipulating the sale of council houses to win votes in marginal wards.

DEATHS
April 25. Lord Killanin, former president of the International Olympic Committee, dies aged 84.

April 27. Cyril Washbrook, England and Lancashire opening batsman from the 1930s to the 1950s, dies aged 84.

LONDON, MONDAY 26

TV presenter Jill Dando shot dead

Jill Dando, 37, at the peak of her television career, planned to marry in September. Her fiancé said she was "admired by all who met her".

Flowers left by admirers in front of Jill Dando's Fulham home, where she died.

One of the best-known figures in British television, BBC presenter Jill Dando, was shot dead on the doorstep of her west London home today. She was 37 years old.

The murder was carried out in broad daylight, at around 11.30 a.m. Dando had just arrived home and was standing at her front door in Gowan Avenue, Fulham, when a man stepped up to her and fired a single bullet at close range into her head. A neighbour found her lying against her front door, with blood pouring from a wound behind her ear. She was certified dead at Charing Cross Hospital at 1 p.m.

The news of Dando's death was received with shock and grief by her many admirers among the TV-viewing public. Some commentators likened the wave of sympathy to that which followed the death of Princess Diana. Both BBC1 and ITV broadcast extended tributes this evening which were watched by millions.

Dando was best known as a co-presenter with Nick Ross of BBC1's *Crimewatch UK*. One theory put forward was that a criminal with a grudge against *Crimewatch UK* might have been behind the killing. Police were also exploring reports that she had complained for some time of being pursued by a stalker.

Dando had planned to marry next September. Her fiancé, Dr Alan Farthing, issued a statement saying: "I am totally devastated and unable to comprehend what has happened. Jill was respected for her professional ability, admired by all who met her, and adored by anyone who got to know her." (→ May 21)

Soho nail bomb causes carnage in gay pub

A bomb exploded in a crowded pub in the centre of London at 6.30 this evening, killing two people and injuring more than 60 others. Two of the injured are critically ill.

The Admiral Duncan pub in Old Compton Street, Soho, is mostly frequented by gays. It was packed with cheerful drinkers on a fine spring evening on the eve of a bank holiday weekend. Eyewitnesses said a young man in a baseball cap left the device in a bag inside the bar. The explosion destroyed the front of the pub. Some of the injured had limbs blown off, while others suffered severe burns and head injuries.

Police are convinced the latest attack is linked to the bombings in Brixton and Brick Lane earlier this month. Sir Paul Condon, the Metropolitan Police commissioner, said the bombings were "most likely the work of far-right extremists targeting minority groups". He described the bombing campaign as "evil" and "an attack on all of us".

Police are looking for a man who was captured on a security camera video shortly before the Brixton bombing two weeks ago. (→ May 2)

Members of the public and the emergency services care for shocked and injured customers of the Admiral Duncan pub after the bomb blast.

Legendary England manager Ramsey is dead

Ramsey was a dour individual, but earned loyalty and respect from his players.

Sir Alf Ramsey, the football manager who won England the World Cup in 1966, died today aged 79.

Ramsey took over as national manager in 1963, after leading lowly Ipswich to the league championship. He brought a new professionalism to the England job, creating a world-beating team out of mostly quite ordinary players.

Ramsey's prickly, remote style won him few friends − he had an outspoken contempt for journalists and foreigners. But his players never questioned his leadership.

His finest moment was at the end of normal time in the World Cup final, when England had just been denied victory by a late German goal. He told his discouraged players: "You've won it once, now you must do it again." And they did.

London, Tuesday 27. Hugh Grant attended the premiere of his new movie *Notting Hill* today with girlfriend Elizabeth Hurley, dressed by Versace.

"James Bond" rides to the rescue of the SNP

Scottish actor Sean Connery, most famous for his role as secret agent James Bond, today intervened in the election campaign for a Scottish parliament, reading a speech in support of the Scottish National Party (SNP).

In a ringing statement of his belief in Scottish independence, Connery declared: "Scotland should be nothing less than equal with all of the other nations of the world."

Almost 20 points behind Labour in the opinion polls, the SNP is in desperate need of a boost from Scotland's most famous celebrity. However, Connery has come under attack in the Scottish press for living safely in the Bahamas while supporting a party committed to raising taxes in Scotland. (→ May 7)

S M T W T F S

S	M	T	W	T	F	S
						1
2	3	4	5	6	7	8
9	10	11	12	13	14	15
16	17	18	19	20	21	22
23	24	25	26	27	28	29
30	31					

Kosovo, 1
According to Serb sources, a Nato attack on a bridge in northern Kosovo hits a bus, killing 40 passengers. (→ May 3)

San Marino, 2
Ferrari driver Michael Schumacher wins the San Marino Grand Prix, taking the lead in this year's Formula One World Championship. (→ May 16)

Celtic Park, 2
Rangers beat Celtic 0-3 to clinch the Scottish Premier League title. The match is marred by crowd violence and three sendings off. (→ May 29)

Macedonia, 3
On an emotional visit to a refugee camp in Macedonia, Tony Blair says of the Kosovo conflict: "This is not a battle for Nato, this is not a battle for territory, this is a battle for humanity." (→ May 6)

Sheffield, 3
Scottish snooker player Stephen Hendry wins the Embassy World Championship for a record seventh time, defeating Mark Williams 18-11 at the Crucible Theatre.

Panama, 3
Panamanians elect their first woman president, Mireya Moscoso, who is the widow of former president, Arnulfo Arias.

London, 4
Railtrack, the company responsible for Britain's surface rail network, says it will bid to take over London Underground.

Bonn, 6
Russia and Nato agree a joint peace plan for Kosovo, involving the deployment of a UN-backed international force to police the province. (→ May 10)

Westminster, 7
The UK Treasury is to sell off 415 tons of its gold reserve in order to buy more foreign currency as investment.

DEATHS

May 2. British actor Oliver Reed, noted for his roles in movies such as *Women in Love* and *The Devils*, dies after collapsing in a bar in Malta, aged 61.

May 3. Godfrey Evans, renowned Kent and England wicketkeeper of the 1940s and 1950s, dies aged 78

May 6. Johnny Morris, presenter of the TV series *Animal Magic* from 1961 to 1983, dies aged 82.

LONDON, SUNDAY 2

Bomb case charge as toll mounts

A man was today charged with three nail-bomb attacks in London over the last fortnight. David Copeland, from Farnborough in Hampshire, was said by police to be a loner with no connection to any neo-Nazi or right-wing extremist group. He was arrested at his home in the early hours of yesterday morning. An officer of Scotland Yard's antiterrorist branch said that some materials found in Copeland's room could have been used for making bombs.

The arrest came only eight hours after the last of the three nail-bomb attacks, which destroyed the Admiral Duncan pub in Soho. Three people have now died as a result of the Soho bomb. Nick Moore, Andrea Dykes, and John Light had stopped at the pub on their way to see a musical. Mrs Dykes was four months pregnant. Her husband, Julian Dykes, and a fifth member of the group, Greg Partridge, are still in a critical condition.

A mourner at a vigil held in Soho two days after the bombing of the Admiral Duncan pub.

Wembley, Saturday 1. In the rugby Silk Cut Challenge Cup final today the Leeds Rhinos defeated the London Broncos by the record margin of 52-16. In a whirlwind finish, Leeds scored six tries in the last 20 minutes. Their winger, Leroy Rivett, became the first player to score four tries in a Wembley final.

London, Saturday 8. Actor Sir Dirk Bogarde has died of a heart attack at the age of 78. Bogarde starred in 70 films, including *Death in Venice*, *The Servant*, **and** *Providence*. **In his later years he also won renown as an author.**

Scotland on course for coalition government

Voters went to the polls yesterday to elect a Scottish parliament, a Welsh assembly, and local councils across Britain. Interest was keenest in Scotland, although even there voter turnout was only 58 per cent. Led by Donald Dewar, Labour emerged on top with 56 seats, but the Scottish Nationalists put in their best-ever performance to take 35 seats. Labour seem sure to form a coalition with the Liberal Democrats − a result of proportional representation.

Labour also led the field in Wales, where only 40 per cent voted. In the local elections, the Tories made sufficient gains to shore up William Hague's leadership. (→ May 12)

Labour's Donald Dewar appears exuberant after yesterday's historic vote in Scotland.

Twisters leave trail of destruction

US soldiers freed after Jackson visit

Three US soldiers held by the Serbs since early April have been freed. Steven Gonzales, Andrew Ramirez, and Christopher Stone were flown to Germany today after civil rights leader Reverend Jesse Jackson went to Belgrade to negotiate their release. Nato sources said, however, that the air campaign against Serbia was set to intensify.

Did Mallory conquer Everest?

The frozen body of British climber George Mallory has been found on Mount Everest 75 years after his bid to conquer the world's highest peak ended in disaster. Accompanied by Andrew Irvine, Mallory attempted the ascent clad in a tweed coat and hobnail boots. It may now be possible to discover whether the pair achieved their goal before they died. Film inside a Kodak camera carried by Mallory on the ascent could show them at the summit.

The wreckage of the town of Moore, Oklahoma, proves the awesome power of the tornado.

The American plains states of Oklahoma and Kansas were today struggling to come to terms with the devastation caused by what were described as the worst tornadoes to hit the US this decade. During last night, entire neighbourhoods were flattened by twisters up to a mile and a half wide, generating wind speeds in excess of 260 mph.

The area that suffered the most damage was around Oklahoma City. The tornado began its course yesterday evening at Chickasha, 50 miles southwest of the city. It progressed steadily northeastward through the night, destroying more than 1,000 homes in Oklahoma City and inflicting widespread destruction on nearby Moore and Del City. Many people took refuge in underground storm shelters, without which casualties would have been far heavier.

One resident said it was "like the Oklahoma City bombing all over again" − a reference to the terrorist attack in 1995 that killed 168 people. So far the death toll in today's natural disaster is 45, but the authorities said that more people could be buried somewhere in the large swathes of splintered wood that are all that is left of what were, until yesterday, thriving neighbourhoods. National Guardsmen have been drafted in to help with the urgent task of searching for survivors.

S	M	T	W	T	F	S
						1
2	3	4	5	6	7	8
9	10	11	12	13	14	15
16	17	18	19	20	21	22
23	24	25	26	27	28	29
30	31					

London, 9
At the annual Bafta TV awards, Dame Thora Hird, 83, wins best actress for her performance in *Waiting for the Telegram* by Alan Bennett. The prize for best soap, a new award this year, is won by *EastEnders*.

Belgrade, 10
The Serb authorities announce that they are ready to carry out a partial withdrawal of their troops from Kosovo. US President Bill Clinton calls the move "encouraging", but Nato airstrikes continue. (→ May 14)

Moscow, 12
President Boris Yeltsin sacks his prime minister, Yevgeny Primakov. It is the third time Yeltsin has dismissed a prime minister in 14 months. (→ August 9)

Westminster, 12
The government announces that it is to put the state-owned betting organization, the Horserace Totalisator Board, better known as the Tote, up for sale.

Cardiff, 12
Alun Michael, the Welsh Labour leader, is elected first secretary of the new Welsh assembly. (→ May 13)

London, 12
A report published in *Nature* magazine says that babies who sleep with a night light in their rooms are five times more likely to be shortsighted in later life.

Edinburgh, 13
After acrimonious negotiations, Labour and the Liberal Democrats agree a deal for a coalition government in Scotland. Scottish Liberal Democrat leader Jim Wallace will be deputy first minister.

Kosovo, 14
Serb television claims that 80 people in the Kosovan village of Korisa have been killed in a Nato air attack. (→ May 27)

Britain, 14
Official figures show that more trains are running late than at any time since the privatization of Britain's railways.

Monte Carlo, 16
In the Formula One championship, Michael Schumacher wins the Monaco Grand Prix ahead of Ferrari colleague Eddie Irvine. (→ June 27)

DEATHS
May 13. Gene Sarazan, a prominent American golfer from the 1920s to the 1950s, dies aged 97.

JERUSALEM, MONDAY 17

Turning point in Israel as Barak triumphs

With returns from Israel's general election still being counted, it is already clear that Labour leader Ehud Barak, aged 57, has scored a landslide victory over the incumbent prime minister, Likud leader Binyamin Netanyahu. Barak looks set to receive about 60 per cent of the votes cast.

The election result is being described by some as a historic turning point for Israel, with a revival of the country's original liberal and secular values. Barak, a retired general and the country's most decorated soldier, tonight promised Israelis "unity and new hope". He is expected to revitalize the flagging Middle East peace process. (→ May 31)

Former soldier Ehud Barak, set to be Israel's next prime minister, embraces a supporter.

Old Trafford, Sunday 16. David Beckham showed off his Premier League champions medal today after Manchester United beat Tottenham 2-1 to take the title by one point over Arsenal. United are also in the FA Cup and European Cup finals. (→ May 22)

SWITZERLAND, WEDNESDAY 12

Names of British spies published on the Net

The names of 115 agents of Britain's Secret Intelligence Service, popularly known as MI6, have been published on the Internet. The British authorities suspect that former MI6 officer Richard Tomlinson, now living in Switzerland, was behind the leak. But Tomlinson, who has already been jailed once for breaking the Official Secrets Act, denies responsibility.

BRISTOL, MONDAY 17

Bookies weep as United win

Kevin McCarron, a student from Bristol, today won £10,764 for a £1 stake after forecasting the winners of all the football divisions in England and Scotland. His bet finally depended on Manchester United, who won the Premiership yesterday. Another punter, who also picked the league winners, won £600,000 for a stake of £130. Bookies now need United to fail in the FA Cup or the European Cup. A United "triple" could cost them £5 million.

Protests rage after Nato missiles hit Chinese embassy building

The Chinese embassy building in Belgrade after Nato's worst "mistake".

Nato was embroiled in a major diplomatic crisis today after an airstrike on Belgrade accidentally hit the Chinese embassy. Chinese protesters have laid siege to the British and American embassies in Beijing, pelting the buildings with stones, burning American flags, and attacking Western journalists.

The airstrike on the Chinese embassy occurred in the early hours of Saturday morning. Three laser-guided missiles hit the building, which had been wrongly identified by the CIA as Serb government offices. The site Nato had intended to destroy was over 180 m away on the opposite side of the same street.

Javier Solana, Nato secretary-general, said that the attack was "a deeply regrettable mistake". Russian leader Boris Yeltsin was less restrained, condemning the Nato error as "an act of vandalism and a flagrant violation of international law".

The incident comes at a sensitive moment during the war in Kosovo, as Russian efforts to broker a peace deal between Nato and Serb leader Slobodan Milosevic appear to be making progress. But Nato leaders feel that the airstrikes are at last forcing Milosevic to seek an end to the war. In a statement today, the Pentagon said: "Nato intends to continue and intensify the air campaign."

The airstrike on the Chinese embassy in Belgrade provoked large-scale protests in Beijing, with the approval of the Chinese authorities.

England open cricket World Cup with a win

The seventh cricket World Cup tournament opened at Lord's today with a lacklustre ceremony and a comfortable victory for England. In traditional English fashion, rain began to fall as the tournament got under way. Some damp fireworks and a flurry of balloons failed to impress the crowd, but England's cricketing performance was more satisfactory. Reigning champions Sri Lanka were all out for 204, a total England's batsmen passed for the loss of only two wickets. With cricketing minnows Kenya and Zimbabwe in their group, England are expected to qualify easily for the next round, the Super Six. (→ May 22)

Prince's friend admits drug use

Tom Parker-Bowles, exposed by Sunday papers for using the illegal drug cocaine.

According to reports in today's *News of the World* and *Sunday Times*, Tom Parker-Bowles, the 24-year-old son of Prince Charles' companion Camilla Parker-Bowles and a close friend of Prince William, has admitted having a cocaine habit.

The young Parker-Bowles was at the Cannes film festival when the admission was made. His friends told the *Sunday Times*: "He is very upset by the whole affair, particularly for dragging his parents into it."

Euthanasia case doctor cleared

Dr David Moor, a 52-year-old family doctor from Fenham, Newcastle upon Tyne, was today cleared of the charge of murdering a patient, 85-year-old George Liddell. Mr Liddell died after Dr Moor administered diamorphine to ease the pain of terminal cancer. Dr Moor argued that he had not practised euthanasia, but had only acted "to relieve agony, distress, and suffering". The law permits such action as long as it does not deliberately hasten death.

London, 18
The Royal Society, Britain's most prestigious scientific body, reports that experiments by Dr Arpad Pusztai, supposedly showing that GM foods had harmful effects on rats, were flawed and unconvincing. (→ May 21)

Malaysia, 20
A cruise ship, the *Sun Vista*, catches fire and sinks off the coast of Malaysia. More than 1,000 passengers and crew take to lifeboats and are rescued.

South Australia, 21
Australian police find eight dismembered bodies in a bank vault in Snowtown, north of Adelaide. Three people have been arrested.

Westminster, 21
The government's chief scientific and medical advisers declare GM foods safe. However, the government announces measures to counter public alarm, including a national scheme to spot any change in patterns of disease. (→ May 27)

New York, 22
A World Health Organization report says that AIDS caused 2.3 million deaths worldwide in 1998. It now kills more people than any other infectious disease.

Wembley, 22
Manchester United beat Newcastle United 2-0 in the FA Cup final through goals by Teddy Sheringham and Paul Scholes. (→ May 26)

Oval, 22
In the cricket World Cup, England are trounced by South Africa. Chasing a total of 226 to win, England's batsmen are all out for 103. (→ May 30)

Westminster, 24
The government publishes a draft version of its proposed Freedom of Information Bill. Critics attack the bill as placing too many restrictions on public access to official documents.

Washington, D.C., 25
A Congressional report states that Chinese spies operating in the United States have stolen nuclear weapons secrets over a 20-year period.

Westminster, 26
The High Court rules that Health Secretary Frank Dobson acted illegally in trying to restrict availability of the anti-impotence drug Viagra on prescription.

Phantom Menace defies critics to break box-office records

American actress Natalie Portman plays Queen Amidala in The Phantom Menace.

The most heavily hyped movie in film industry history opened yesterday across the United States. *Star Wars: Episode 1 – The Phantom Menace* was panned by most critics, but fans of George Lucas's *Star Wars* series queued for days before the opening to snap up first-day tickets.

The result is that the movie has already broken its first box-office record by taking $28.5 million (£18 million) on its first day. The previous record was held by the sequel to *Jurassic Park, The Lost World*, which took $26 million in 1997.

The Phantom Menace stars Ewan McGregor and Liam Neeson, but the real pull of the movie lies in the spectacular special effects. The film will open in Britain in July.

DJ rapist may have attacked 50 women

Richard Baker, 34, from Bodmin, Cornwall, has been convicted of 12 sex attacks, including three rapes and seven indecent assaults. Describing Baker as "one of the most prolific sex offenders this country has ever seen", police said he may have carried out over 50 attacks on women.

Handsome and outwardly charming, Baker worked as a DJ in the south of Spain. He is believed to have raped young tourists, using a "date-rape drug" to make them helpless.

Labour MPs stage benefit revolt

The government's majority of 176 in the House of Commons was cut to 40 last night as 67 Labour MPs voted against proposed changes to disability benefits contained in the Welfare Reform Bill. At least 15 other Labour members abstained.

Prime Minister Tony Blair has given the bill his full backing, and a Downing Street source described the welfare reforms as "principled and right". (→ October 13)

London, Wednesday 26. Artist David Hockney today unveiled to a crowded press room his latest works, which will be shown at the Royal Academy summer exhibition. He said his huge, colourful paintings of the Grand Canyon expressed his "love of open spaces".

New poet laureate is greeted with sneers and jeers

Oxford-educated poet and biographer Andrew Motion is to succeed the late Ted Hughes as poet laureate. The news of the appointment was today greeted with derision by some of his fellow versifiers. One poet, who was not named, said the choice was "a disgrace, a scandal, and an insult to the country's intelligence".

The poet laureate is appointed by the Queen but chosen by the prime minister. Motion put himself in line for the post with a moving poem on the death of Princess Diana in 1997.

Jill Dando is buried – her death still an enigma

Jill Dando's coffin is carried out of a Baptist chapel in Weston-super-Mare for burial.

The funeral of murdered TV presenter Jill Dando took place today in her home town, the Somerset seaside resort of Weston-super-Mare.

Among the mourners at the funeral were her fiancé, Dr Alan Farthing, many leading TV personalities, and singer Sir Cliff Richard, one of Dando's closest friends. The Reverend Roger Collins told the congregation inside Clarence Road Baptist Church that "when Jill was shot, a lively, loving, beautiful light was extinguished".

Police say they have made progress in identifying the kind of gun used in the killing, but they have not yet established a credible motive. (→ August 21)

England captain resigns over drug allegations

Lawrence Dallaglio resigned today as England rugby captain after the *News of the World* said it had recorded statements in which he admitted using and dealing in illegal drugs. According to Dallaglio, reporters posing as business executives offering sponsorship raised the subject of drugs and he foolishly "created stories which were simply not true" to impress them. (→ July 19)

United triumph on night of drama

Manchester United goalkeeper Peter Schmeichel leads the celebrations after his side's extraordinary last-minute victory over Bayern.

Alex Ferguson enjoys his finest hour.

Manchester United tonight defeated Bayern Munich 2-1 to win the European Cup after one of the most startling comebacks in footballing history. The English side seemed to be drifting to defeat after going a goal behind to a soft free kick early in the game. A minute into injury time, however, Teddy Sheringham scored from a corner by David Beckham. Less than a minute later, another Beckham corner was turned in by Ole Gunnar Solskjaer, and Manchester had won.

The match was watched by a crowd of 90,000 in Nou Camp stadium, Barcelona, and by an estimated 500 million television viewers across the world. The victory meant Manchester had achieved a unique treble, as they had already won the Premiership and the FA Cup. The club had only won the top European competition once before, in 1968.

The occasion was a personal triumph for manager Alex Ferguson, who always said his career would be incomplete without a victory in Europe. After the match, Ferguson admitted that he had thought his team were beaten. "What they have achieved is unprecedented," he said. "Nobody has ever done it. They deserve it." (→ June 11)

S	M	T	W	T	F	S
						1
2	3	4	5	6	7	8
9	10	11	12	13	14	15
16	17	18	19	20	21	22
23	24	25	26	27	28	29
30	31					

The Hague, 27
A warrant for the arrest of President Slobodan Milosevic and four other Serb leaders is issued by the International War Crimes Tribunal for Former Yugoslavia. They are charged with crimes against humanity, including murder, persecution, and mass deportations. (→ June 4)

London, 27
Eddie George, the governor of the Bank of England, tells a House of Commons committee that he is unsure whether Britain is ready to adopt the euro.

Milan, 28
Leonardo da Vinci's *Last Supper* is put on show to the public again in the Convent of Santa Maria delle Grazie following 20 years of controversial restoration work.

Westminster, 29
James Major, son of former prime minister John Major, marries ex-model Emma Noble in the crypt chapel at the Houses of Parliament. (→ July 20)

Hampden Park, 29
Rangers beat traditional rivals Celtic 1-0 in the Scottish Cup final, with Rod Wallace scoring the winning goal.

Jerusalem, 29
Orthodox Jews protest at the holding of the Eurovision Song Contest in Israel. They are angry that a dress rehearsal takes place on a Saturday, claiming it is a "desecration of the sabbath".

Salzburg, 29
Flames sweep through the Tauern tunnel in the Austrian Alps, killing at least four people and forcing hundreds to flee.

Istanbul, 31
Turkey puts the Kurdish rebel leader Abdullah Ocalan on trial for treason. Ocalan has called for peace, but claims that if he is sentenced to death, the rebellion will continue. (→ June 29)

Lebanon, 31
The Israeli-backed South Lebanese Army starts to withdraw from Israel's "security zone" in southern Lebanon. Israel's new prime minister, Ehud Barak, promised during his election campaign to end the Israeli presence in Lebanon within a year.

Minsk, 31
A storm during an open-air festival in Minsk, the capital of Belarus, causes a stampede in which 50 teenagers and three police officers are crushed to death.

India's Anil Kumble dismisses Andy Flintoff during England's batting debacle.

EDGBASTON, SUNDAY 30
England shamed by World Cup exit

Holding the cricket World Cup in England was supposed to be a chance for the national team to reverse its recent record of failure. But today, chasing an Indian total of 233, England were bowled out for 169, ending their chances of qualifying for the next round, the Super Six. They came fourth in their group, behind South Africa, India, and Zimbabwe.

Tournament organizer Michael Browning said England's early exit was "the nightmare scenario". The future of Alec Stewart as England captain is now in doubt. (→ June 17)

IRELAND, SUNDAY 30
Anger over search for IRA victims' bodies

As part of the Northern Ireland peace process, the IRA has started returning the bodies of some of its victims to their families. On Friday, the remains of Eamon Molloy, an alleged informer who disappeared in 1975, were left in a coffin at Faughart graveyard near Dundalk.

The IRA has also given details of where eight other "disappeared" victims are buried. However, excavations by Irish police have so far failed to locate any more bodies. Public anger is growing as details of the 1970s killings come to light, and victims' families endure the agonizing wait for news. (→ June 29)

INDIAN OCEAN, THURSDAY 27
Lost continent found under ocean

Researchers announced today that they have discovered a lost continent under the southern Indian Ocean.

They claim that the Kerguelen Plateau, now more than 1,800 m under the sea, was once a land mass covered with ferns and conifers. It sank beneath the waves 20 million years ago, but drilling by geologists has located seeds and pollen buried in rock layers on the ocean floor.

Outer Space, Monday 31. Astronauts from the shuttle *Discovery* today attached a crane to an orbiting module in the latest phase of construction of the International Space Station (ISS).

Climbdown by Sun editor over use of Sophie topless shot

Sophie Rhys-Jones at the wedding of her dress designer Samantha Shaw.

TOPLESS
Star Tarrant's sexy fun with Edward's bride

The front page of the offending issue of the Sun. *The more revealing image appeared inside.*

The *Sun* newspaper today said sorry for publishing a topless photo of Sophie Rhys-Jones, who is due to marry Prince Edward next month. The newspaper's editor, David Yelland, also made a public personal apology, admitting that the use of the picture had caused "great distress".

The photograph, taken in Spain 11 years ago when Rhys-Jones was a PR officer with Capital Radio, shows her in the back seat of a car with disc jockey Chris Tarrant. He had pulled at her bikini top as a practical joke, exposing one breast. The picture was taken by Kara Noble, now a radio presenter. She sold the photograph to the *Sun* for a reported £200,000.

Tarrant said he was "totally sickened" by the use of the photograph, and was adamant there was never "the slightest hint of romance" between himself and Rhys-Jones. A Buckingham Palace spokesman said that a formal complaint was being lodged against the *Sun* for a gross invasion of privacy.

Rhys-Jones today attended the wedding of dress designer Samantha Shaw. Her only comment to the press was: "Let's move on." (→ June 2)

GM foods "needed to feed the hungry"

An independent think-tank, the Nuffield Council on Bioethics, said today that there were compelling moral reasons for developing GM (genetically modified) crops. The Nuffield report, which took 18 months to produce, argues that GM foods are needed to fight world hunger. It concedes, however, that consumers should have the right to avoid GM foods if they wish.

The government welcomed the report. Prime Minister Tony Blair attacked the media for failing to give adequate coverage to such expert opinion, instead reporting "anything which fed hysteria". (→ July 18)

Aircraft shot down in border war

Indian troops standing guard along the disputed Kashmir border with Pakistan.

Pakistan's smouldering conflict with India over the disputed territory of Kashmir burst into open warfare yesterday when an Indian MiG fighter was shot down by a Pakistani surface-to-air missile. Indian aircraft were flying ground-attack missions against Pakistani-backed Islamic guerrillas operating on the Indian side of the Kashmir border.

An Indian officer, Air Commodore Subash Bhojwani, told the press: "This is war. There is no intention of a let-up in the airstrikes."

The potential seriousness of the conflict was underlined today as Pakistan held a rally to celebrate the anniversary of its first nuclear weapons test last year. India, too, has its own nuclear armoury. (→ July 12)

S	M	T	W	T	F	S
		1	2	3	4	5
6	7	8	9	10	11	12
13	14	15	16	17	18	19
20	21	22	23	24	25	26
27	28	29	30			

Brussels, 1
Belgian chickens and eggs are banned in Europe for fear they may be contaminated with a cancer-causing dioxin.

Edinburgh, 2
The Bank of Scotland drops a planned partnership with the American television evangelist Pat Robertson after he says that Scotland is overrun by homosexuals and could "go right back to the darkness".

London, 2
The Press Complaints Commission criticizes *Sun* editor David Yelland for publishing a topless photograph of Sophie Rhys-Jones. (→ June 19)

Wembley, 5
Paul Scholes is sent off as England draw 0-0 with Sweden in a European Championship qualifier. (→ June 9)

Portadown, 5
A 59-year-old mother of two, Elizabeth O'Neill, is killed when a Loyalist bomb is thrown into her home. (→ June 22)

Lausanne, 7
Irish swimmer Michelle Smith loses her appeal in the Court of Arbitration for Sport against a four-year suspension for using a banned anabolic steroid.

Old Bailey, 8
Former Tory minister Jonathan Aitken is sentenced to 18 months for perjury. The offence was committed during a failed libel case against *The Guardian* in 1997.

Sofia, 9
England look unlikely to qualify for soccer's European Championship after a 1-1 draw with Bulgaria. (→ September 9)

London, 9
BBC1 scraps *The Vanessa Show*, presented by Vanessa Feltz, after poor ratings and a scandal over fake guests.

City of London, 10
The Bank of England cuts the base rate of interest to 5 per cent, its lowest level for 22 years. (→ September 8)

Leeds, 11
Tony Benn's son Hilary wins the Leeds Central by-election for Labour, but voter turnout, 19.6 per cent, hits a 50-year low.

DEATHS
June 1. Sir Christopher Cockerell, inventor of the hovercraft, dies aged 88.

June 12. DeForest Kelley, who played Dr McCoy in *Star Trek*, dies aged 79.

BELGRADE, FRIDAY 4

Peace deal on Kosovo, but bombing goes on

Kosovans released from a Serb internment camp during the peace negotiations express a range of emotions, from relief to anguish.

The Serb parliament today voted to accept peace terms proposed jointly by Russia and the European Union, opening up the prospect of a rapid end to the war over Kosovo. The terms were delivered to the Serb capital, Belgrade, by Russian envoy Viktor Chernomyrdin and Finnish President Martti Ahtisaari, acting for the EU. There is to be an immediate end to "violence and repression" in Kosovo, and Serb forces are to withdraw from the province. Kosovo will then be occupied by an international force under the command of Nato. Finally, all Kosovan refugees are to be allowed to return to their homes.

However, Nato sources said that the bombing would continue until Serb leaders had agreed the details of the military withdrawal. (→ June 13)

LONDON, FRIDAY 11

Knighthoods for Trevor and Alex

Sir Trevor McDonald, one of Britain's most popular and respected TV personalities.

"Stunned but absolutely delighted" was how veteran newscaster Trevor McDonald described his reaction when he learned today that he had been awarded a knighthood in the Queen's Birthday Honours. Sir Trevor began his career as a journalist in his native Trinidad. When he joined ITN in 1973, he was the network's first black reporter.

Also knighted was Manchester United's manager, Alex Ferguson. He celebrated the news with champagne in the south of France.

BRITAIN, SUNDAY 13

Boost for Tories as voters turn their backs on Europe

The Conservative Party won nationwide elections today for the first time since 1992 – despite opinion polls consistently putting the Tories behind Labour by around 20 per cent. The elections, for representatives to sit in the European parliament, gave the Conservatives 36 seats to Labour's 29.

But Britain's first nationwide exercise in proportional representation attracted an unprecedentedly low voter turnout: only 23 per cent of the electorate voted. As the most successful party, the Tories still only won the votes of 8.3 per cent of electors.

The elections are being interpreted above all as a statement of popular indifference or even hostility towards Europe, and especially towards monetary union. The result is bound to encourage the anti-European tendency among the Tories.

KOSOVO, SUNDAY 13

Nato and Russian troops occupy Kosovo

British tanks roll towards Pristina, greeted with V-for-victory signs by enthusiastic Kosovans, who regarded the troops as liberators from Serb violence and oppression.

British troops are patrolling the bomb-scarred streets of the Kosovan capital, Pristina, today as part of K-For, the international force sent in to implement the Kosovo peace accord. Some of the 5,000-strong British unit arrived in armoured columns from Macedonia, while others were flown in by helicopter. They have been greeted by ethnic Albanians as saviours after the nightmare of Serb ethnic cleansing.

It is four days since Serb generals agreed a military pact with Nato detailing the terms of their withdrawal from Kosovo, but there was a delay in Nato forces moving into the province, apparently so that US troops could appear in the first wave. As a result of the delay, Russian forces arrived in Pristina first, on Friday. They were welcomed by the Serbs, who see them as allies against Nato and the ethnic Albanians.

Nato is playing down the incident with Russia, however, since Russian participation is an essential part of the peace accord. (→ June 16)

Paris, Sunday 6. American tennis star Andre Agassi was overcome by emotion today after coming back from two sets down to win the French Open. He has now won all four tennis "grand slam" titles.

SOUTH AFRICA, THURSDAY 3

Mbeki is successor to Mandela

As votes are counted in South Africa's second multiracial democratic elections, it is already certain that the ruling African National Congress (ANC) will remain in power with an overwhelming majority.

The new ANC leader, Thabo Mbeki, will take over from Nelson Mandela as South Africa's president when Mandela retires in two weeks' time. In his victory speech today, Mbeki declared: "Our people, both black and white, have mandated us to pursue our goal of a non-racial South Africa." (→ June 16)

Thabo Mbeki on the campaign trail.

Britain, 14
American retailer Wal-Mart announces it is buying the British supermarket chain Asda. The arrival of Wal-Mart, with its slogan "We sell for less, always", is expected to spark a retail price war.

Westminster, 14
The government announces a £60 million plan to halve the rate of teenage pregnancies. Britain's teenage birth rate is currently the highest in Europe.

Luxembourg, 15
EU agriculture ministers agree that battery farming of chickens is to be banned. Farmers will have until 2012 to change to free-range or cages that meet new standards.

Westminster, 15
In a reshuffle of the shadow cabinet, William Hague sacks his deputy leader, Peter Lilley, who had enraged many Tories with a call to end Thatcherism. Ann Widdecombe is promoted to shadow home secretary.

Athens, 16
American athlete Maurice Greene sets a new world 100 m record of 9.79 seconds.

Britain, 16
Former Formula One champion driver Damon Hill says he is retiring from motor racing at the end of the current season.

Pretoria, 16
In a moving ceremony, Nelson Mandela steps down as president of South Africa. He is succeeded by Thabo Mbeki.

Westminster, 17
The government announces it has shelved controversial proposals for a new system of "no fault" divorce.

Cologne, 18
Meeting in Germany, the G7 group of top industrial nations agrees a $100 billion (£60 billion) programme of debt relief for the world's poorest countries.

Old Bailey, 18
Nightclub DJ Richard Baker is given four life sentences for rape and other sex offences. The judge, Recorder David Stokes, calls him "depraved and wicked".

DEATHS
June 16. David Edward Sutch, better known as Screaming Lord Sutch, founder of the Official Monster Raving Loony Party, dies by hanging himself at his home in Harrow, aged 58.

Kosovan refugees hurry home

Nato said that it fought the war against Serbia so that the Kosovans could return safely to their homes. Today that pledge was being fulfilled. Thousand upon thousand of refugees, driven from Kosovo by the Serbs, are leaving camps in Albania and Macedonia to trek back to their abandoned towns and villages.

UNHCR, the UN refugee agency supervising resettlement, has been overwhelmed by the speed of the exodus; it had thought that fear would make the refugees hesitate to go back.

Most are returning to ruined houses and to lives scarred by the loss of loved ones. But today they waved, smiled, and sang, just glad to be going home. (→ June 18)

Kosovan refugees were united in joy at their return from forced exile.

Serb soldiers were on their guard, fearful of revenge attacks by angry ethnic Albanians.

Political chaos in Kosovo as Nato struggles to get a grip

Nato forces, under the command of General Sir Michael Jackson, are squaring up to the immense task of restoring peace and security in the chaos that engulfs Kosovo.

Today, in the southern town of Prizren, German Nato forces found a torture chamber being run by the Kosovo Liberation Army (KLA), which is bent on revenge against Serbs and those who collaborated with them during the war.

At the same time, in the north of the province, Serb troops withdrawing from Kosovo were blatantly burning buildings and destroying secret files under the eyes of Nato troops. Evidence of Serb atrocities is mounting with every day that passes, further fuelling ethnic hatreds that make Kosovo ungovernable.

However, there was a step forward today when Nato and Russia agreed on the role to be played by Russian troops in the area. Five Russian battalions will operate independently alongside Nato forces. (→ June 21)

CITY OF LONDON, FRIDAY 18

Carnival turns to riot as anti-capitalists take on the City

This was the day when, in the words of *The Times*, "pin-stripes met pins-in-the-nose", as some 3,000 assorted anarchists, animal rights activists, and environmentalists besieged the banks and investment houses of the City of London. They were responding to a call by a group named J18 for "a day of international action, protest, and carnival against capitalism".

At the beginning, the carnival atmosphere was pervasive. Protesters danced outside City buildings, banging drums and blowing whistles. But the atmosphere changed after a demonstrator was knocked down by a police van. Protesters went on the rampage, smashing windows, trashing restaurants, and irrupting into office buildings. Police counter-attacked in force, and running battles developed in side streets.

By the time order returned, 46 people had been injured. The cost of damage to property is estimated at more than £1 million. (→ July 28)

The early stages of the anti-capitalist carnival were colourful and good humoured, but violent scenes followed later in the day.

LONDON, THURSDAY 17

Death of "a true holy man"

Cardinal Hume, Catholic spiritual leader.

The Archbishop of Westminster, Cardinal Basil Hume, died of cancer tonight in a London hospital. He was 76 years old. During his 23 years in the Westminster see, Cardinal Hume was recognized as a spiritual leader by people of all faiths. The Queen was said to be "deeply saddened" by his death, and Prime Minister Tony Blair described him as "goodness personified, a true holy man".

Windsor, Saturday 19. Prince Edward and Sophie Rhys-Jones were married in informal style at St George's Chapel today. The wedding was held at 5 p.m. and guests were asked not to wear hats. The royal couple will henceforth be known as the Earl and Countess of Wessex.

BRITAIN, TUESDAY 15

Gay Boyzone star goes public

Stephen Gately of the immensely successful Irish band Boyzone today revealed that he is a homosexual. Gately, 23, is an idol for thousands of teenage girls. He said: "Many of them may be upset. I only hope they understand how important it is for me to reveal that I am gay." Gately decided to go public after learning that he was about to be "outed".

EDGBASTON, THURSDAY 17

World Cup classic puts Aussies in final

Australia are through to the cricket World Cup final on run rate, after tying with South Africa in a memorable semifinal. The South Africans began the last over needing nine runs to win with one wicket standing. Lance Klusener hit fours off the first two balls, but was run out going for the winning single. Australia will face Pakistan in the final. (→ June 20)

S	M	T	W	T	F	S
		1	2	3	4	5
6	7	8	9	10	11	12
13	14	15	16	17	18	19
20	21	22	23	24	25	26
27	28	29	30			

Kosovo, 21
Two Gurkhas serving with the Royal Engineers are killed by an explosion, the first Nato fatalities in Kosovo. (→ June 23)

Westminster, 22
The government proposes to set learning goals for young children. By the age of six, they should be able to count to ten, recite the alphabet, and read some words.

London, 22
Prime Minister Tony Blair queries the value of motorway bus lanes after being caught in a traffic jam on the M4 where a bus-lane project is being tested. Blair's car uses the bus lane to escape the jam.

Berlin, 23
Sir Simon Rattle is appointed conductor of the Berlin Philharmonic, arguably the world's most prestigious orchestra.

Lord's, 23
Indian-born Nasser Hussain is chosen as England's new cricket captain and Duncan Fletcher as the new coach. (→ July 25)

Winsford, Cheshire, 23
A Euston-to-Glasgow express ploughs into a commuter train that has passed a red signal. Prompt braking by the express driver prevents loss of life.

Magny-Cours, France, 27
German driver Heinz-Harald Frentzen wins the Formula One French Grand Prix for Jordan. (→ July 11)

Northern Ireland, 28
Loyalists express outrage as the Parades Commission bans the Orange Order's annual Drumcree march. (→ July 15)

Istanbul, 29
A Turkish court sentences Kurdish rebel leader Abdullah Ocalan to death.

Ireland, 29
After a four-week search in a bog, police find the bodies of two IRA victims, John McClory and Brian McKinney, killed 21 years ago. The IRA had indicated where the men were buried as part of the move to return the bodies of the "disappeared".

Wimbledon, 30
Tim Henman reaches the quarter finals of the men's singles, beating American Jim Courier in five sets. But Britain's other tennis ace, Greg Rusedski, is beaten by Australian Mark Philippoussis. (→ July 4)

Europe, 30
Duty-free shopping is abolished for travellers within the European Union.

BELFAST, TUESDAY 22
Release of bomber fuels Ulster crisis

At 11 o'clock this morning, IRA terrorist Patrick Magee walked out of the Maze prison to freedom. Magee was the man who, in 1984, planted the bomb that nearly killed Margaret Thatcher, then prime minister, at the Grand Hotel in Brighton. Two years later he was sentenced to a minimum of 35 years in jail for the murder of the five people who died in the bombing. But, released under the terms of last year's Good Friday agreement, Magee has served less than 14 years.

Unionists have attacked the British government for releasing paramilitary prisoners while the IRA still resists moves towards disarmament. Unionist leader David Trimble today called for the sacking of Northern Ireland Secretary Mo Mowlam, claiming she had lost the confidence of his party. Meanwhile, Prime Minister Tony Blair acknowledged that the Good Friday accord was close to collapse. If it did, he said, we will "just have to pick up the pieces in the best way we can". (→ June 28)

LONDON, THURSDAY 24
Tories talk of "cronyism" as Dyke takes over at the BBC

A cheerful Greg Dyke, soon to be in charge of the BBC after a hard-fought political battle.

Greg Dyke, chairman of Pearson Television and a wealthy Labour supporter, has been selected as the new director-general of the BBC. Making the announcement today, the BBC Board of Governors said that Dyke had the "skills, flair, and experience to lead the BBC forward."

Dyke's candidacy had been hotly opposed by Tory leader William Hague, who saw it as an example of "Labour cronyism". Dyke is known to have made a £50,000 contribution to Labour Party funds. He has, however, pledged to uphold the Corporation's political independence.

Lord's, Sunday 20. Australia's cricketers today celebrated winning the World Cup with a crushing victory in the final against Pakistan. Leg-spinner Shane Warne (above centre) was made man of the match for taking four wickets as Pakistan were bowled out for 132, a total that Australia passed in just 20 overs.

Wimbledon, Tuesday 22. In one of the biggest upsets in tennis history, 16-year-old Australian Jelena Dokic today defeated top seed Martina Hingis in the opening game of the Wimbledon women's singles. Dokic, 129th in the world rankings, won 6-2, 6-0. (→ June 30)

WESTMINSTER, TUESDAY 29

Jack Straw in the firing line as passport queues lengthen

Home Secretary Jack Straw today apologized for a crisis at the Passport Agency that has left a backlog of 565,000 applications waiting to be processed. Thousands of people have had to go in person to the passport office in Petty France, Westminster, and queue for hours to get a passport in time for their trip abroad.

Straw blamed the crisis on increased demand, especially due to the introduction of compulsory passports for children, and on problems with a new computer system. Mike O'Brien, a Home Office minister, admitted the crisis had put ministers' jobs "on the line". (→ July 1)

Home Secretary Straw under pressure.

MANCHESTER, WEDNESDAY 30

United to swap the FA Cup for Brazil trip

Manchester United agreed today to withdraw from this season's FA Cup competition, so that they can play in the first World Club Championship in Brazil next January. Manager Sir Alex Ferguson said he was "disappointed", but there was no choice.

The government and the FA had urged Manchester to take part in the new competition, since their participation will aid England's bid to host the 2006 World Cup. Many fans see it as another step in the gradual downgrading of domestic football in favour of lucrative international tournaments "made for television".

NEW YORK, FRIDAY 25

Swift remarriage for Murdoch

Two weeks after the legal end of his 32-year marriage to Anna Murdoch, media billionaire Rupert Murdoch today married Wendy Deng, 32, at a private ceremony on board his yacht moored off Manhattan. His new wife is an executive of Star TV, a Hong Kong subsidiary of Murdoch's global media empire. It is 68-year-old Murdoch's third marriage.

KOSOVO, WEDNESDAY 23

British investigators in gruesome Kosovo massacre probe

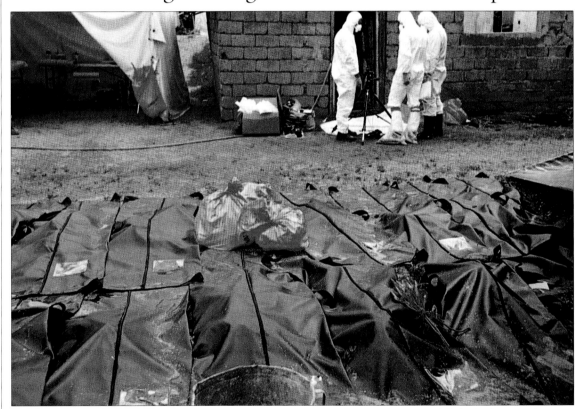

Body bags laid out in a courtyard hold the remains of massacre victims, as experts in protective clothing search for further forensic evidence.

The reality of Serb atrocities in Kosovo is being revealed as forensic experts sift gruesome evidence at sites now under Nato control.

At a burnt-out farmhouse in the village of Velika Krusa, rows of body bags in the farm courtyard contain the remains of 40 bodies identified by British police and forensic experts working for the International War Crimes Tribunal. The police believe that the victims were herded into the farm and killed with machine-gun fire. The building was then set on fire by the Serbs to hide evidence.

Foreign Secretary Robin Cook today visited the site and called on those who doubted the morality of the Nato military campaign to "come and look at what we have found". (→ July 9)

S	M	T	W	T	F	S
				1	2	3
4	5	6	7	8	9	10
11	12	13	14	15	16	17
18	19	20	21	22	23	24
25	26	27	28	29	30	31

Westminster, 1
The government announces emergency measures to cope with the passport crisis. People waiting to renew passports will be given a two-year extension at post offices.

London, 2
The High Court dismisses manslaughter charges against driver Larry Harrison and Great Western Trains, who were charged over the 1997 Southall rail crash, in which seven people died after an express passed a red signal. (→ September 20)

Stamford Bridge, 5
Chelsea Football Club sign striker Chris Sutton from Blackburn for £10 million.

Westminster, 6
Prime Minister Tony Blair says that he bears "scars on his back" from fighting public sector workers over modernization. The outburst follows criticism of the government by doctors.

Rome, 7
Moroccan runner Hicham El Guerrouj sets a new world record for the mile at 3 minutes 43.13 seconds.

London, 8
Speaking on BBC1's *Question Time*, Tony Blair pledges to outlaw hunting with dogs before the next election.

Britain, 8
Writing in the *British Medical Journal*, Dr Andrew Ness praises the medical benefits of sunlight, criticizing the current stress on the risk of skin cancer.

Kosovo, 9
Nato troops find about 350 bodies in a ravine outside Ljubenic, victims of a massacre by Serb paramilitaries and police last April. (→ July 16)

Brussels, 9
Former Labour leader Neil Kinnock is appointed vice-president of the European Commission, with special responsibility for administrative reform.

DEATHS
July 1. Joshua Nkomo, a leader in the struggle for black majority rule in Zimbabwe, dies aged 82.

July 2. Mario Puzo, Italian-American author of *The Godfather,* dies on Long Island, New York, aged 78.

July 6. Joaquin Rodrigo, Spanish composer famous for his *Concierto de Aranjuez* for guitar and orchestra, dies aged 97.

EDINBURGH, THURSDAY 1

Queen opens Scottish parliament

The first Scottish parliament for 292 years was opened by the Queen in Edinburgh's Assembly Hall today. Defying media predictions of popular apathy, Scots turned out in large numbers to celebrate the occasion, cheering the royal procession.

There was one difficult moment during the procession, however, when a group of pro-Irish nationalist protesters jumped crash barriers and rushed the Queen's carriage, but they were easily restrained.

In her address, the Queen spoke of "a moment, rare in the life of any nation, when we step across the threshold of a new constitutional age". She praised the Scots' "grit, determination, and humour", and declared confidence in their future.

Traditional singer Sheena Wellington sang Robert Burns's "A Man's a Man for A' That", with everyone joining in the chorus, and a humorous poem by 11-year-old Amy Linekar, called "How to Create a Great Country", was read to fine effect.

The overall impression was that the day went remarkably well. Now the politicians have to take over.

The Queen rides in an open carriage from the Palace of Holyroodhouse to the Assembly Hall, flanked by the Household Cavalry.

BRITAIN, THURSDAY 1

Tory era ends as Willie Whitelaw dies

Viscount Whitelaw of Penrith, a former Tory minister, died last night at the age of 81. As William Whitelaw, he served loyally under both Edward Heath and Margaret Thatcher. He was Thatcher's deputy for eight years – she once said, with unintentional humour, "every prime minister needs a Willie".

Whitelaw was a Tory of the old school, noted for a mild, bumbling style. His instinctive response to any remark was "splendid, splendid". But outward vagueness masked an astute sense of politics. He once wrote: "It is never wise to appear more clever than you are. It is sometimes wise to appear slightly less so."

Viscount Whitelaw, cleverer than he seemed.

ILLINOIS, MONDAY 5

Race–hate killer a "martyr", says Church chief

A man who killed two people and injured seven others in a racially motivated shooting spree over the Independence Day holiday was today described as a "martyr for free speech". The claim was made by Matt Hale, head of the white supremacist World Church of the Creator. Hale said that Benjamin Smith, 21, a former member of the church, had been incensed by censorship of his racist views. Smith killed himself in Salem, Illinois, after being pursued by police in a car chase.

American tennis triumph on Independence Day

Lindsay Davenport and Pete Sampras make the patriotic point after their victories.

British tennis fans had hoped that today would see Tim Henman compete in his first Wimbledon final. But instead, two American players celebrated Independence Day in style.

After dismissing Henman in the semifinal, Pete Sampras dispatched his more glamorous compatriot, Andre Agassi, 6-3, 6-4, 7-5 in a one-sided final. The quiet American has now surpassed many more flamboyant figures to become the only man in the 20th century to win six Wimbledon singles titles.

In the women's singles, there was no romantic ending for 30-year-old former champion Steffi Graf. She announced her retirement after a final in which she lost in straight sets to America's Lindsay Davenport.

Rogue trader Leeson comes home

Nick Leeson is escorted through Heathrow airport after flying back from Singapore. He was released from Tanah Merah prison on June 30.

Notorious futures trader Nick Leeson landed at Heathrow today after his release from the Singapore jail where he has been a prisoner for the last four years. Leeson's illegal dealings ruined his employers, Barings Bank, by losing them an estimated £850 million.

At a press conference, Leeson said he was looking forward to ordinary things "like being able to have a cup of tea or a drink with my mates". He was operated on for cancer during his time in prison and his life is still at risk. His financial assets have been frozen by creditors of Barings, but he has sold his story to the *Daily Mail* for an alleged sum of over £100,000.

Posh and Beckham marry in gaudy style

Footballer David Beckham married Posh Spice Victoria Adams in regal style at 15th-century Luttrellstown Castle outside Dublin today.

The ceremony, attended by a select group of family and friends, was conducted by the Bishop of Cork in a chapel in the castle battlements. Beckham's best man was fellow United player Gary Neville.

The couple then moved to a marquee in the castle grounds for the lavish reception. They welcomed their 236 guests with their baby, Brooklyn, in a crib alongside them. Food served at the supper that followed ranged from red pepper soup and summer berry terrine to the groom's favourite, toffee pudding.

Gilt props are removed after the wedding.

The media were clamouring for a glimpse of the gaudy details of the wedding, such as Victoria's gold and diamond coronet, the red velvet thrones the couple sat on, and their personal coat of arms unveiled after the ceremony. But tight security, including a flight exclusion zone around the area imposed by the Irish authorities, ensured that only *OK!* magazine had photos of the event.

S	M	T	W	T	F	S
				1	2	3
4	5	6	7	8	9	10
11	12	13	14	15	16	17
18	19	20	21	22	23	24
25	26	27	28	29	30	31

Israel, 11
New Israeli Prime Minister Ehud Barak has his first meeting with Palestinian leader Yassir Arafat. Barak agrees to implement a deal that will give the Palestinian Authority greater autonomy and control of more territory.

Pakistan, 12
Pakistani Prime Minister Nawaz Sharif says that he has averted a nuclear conflict by making a deal with India to defuse tension on the Kashmir border. Pakistani-backed Muslim fighters are to withdraw from Indian territory. (→ October 12)

London, 13
Detective Inspector Ben Bullock, the only police officer involved in the botched Stephen Lawrence murder investigation to face a disciplinary hearing, is found guilty of two minor acts of negligence. Stephen's mother, Doreen Lawrence, describes the hearing as a "whitewash".

Tehran, 13
Iranian students demanding democratic reforms riot in the capital, Tehran. Rioters are fired on by police and by pro-government vigilantes.

Brussels, 14
British Airways is fined £4 million by the European Commission for providing "anti-competitive" incentives to travel agents to steer their customers onto BA flights. BA says it will appeal.

New York, 16
Microsoft becomes the first company in the world to be valued at over $500 billion (£300 billion) as its share price rises in the wake of a successful law suit.

Kosovo, 16
UNHCR, the United Nations refugee agency, says that revenge attacks by ethnic Albanians are threatening to drive all Serbs out of Kosovo. It is estimated that almost 150,000 Kosovan Serbs have fled to Serbia since the war ended. (→ July 24)

Paris, 17
Renowned Spanish fashion designer Paco Rabanne gives his last Paris show. He claims to be fleeing the city because it is about to be destroyed by the Russian space station *Mir* falling from the sky.

DEATHS
July 12. Bill Owen, the actor who played Compo in the BBC's long-running comedy series *Last of the Summer Wine*, dies of cancer aged 85.

LONDON, FRIDAY 16
Blair wins press complaint ruling over children

The Press Complaints Commission today ruled that articles published in the *Mail on Sunday* last January invaded the privacy of Prime Minister Tony Blair's 11-year-old daughter, Kathryn.

Tony and Cherie Blair lodged a complaint about the articles, which suggested that their daughter had received special treatment in being awarded a place at a popular west London school. The commission ruled that the articles misleadingly repeated unsubstantiated allegations by local parents, and served no "exceptional public interest".

It was the first time that a serving prime minister had complained to the commission, and the first time a complaint had been brought under new rules designed to protect the privacy of famous people's children.

Lake Constance, Saturday 17. This year's Bregenz Festival includes a version of Verdi's opera *Un Ballo in Maschera*, performed on a stage consisting of a vast 50-ton floating book watched over by death.

MASSACHUSETTS, SATURDAY 17
JFK Jr missing, feared dead

A light aircraft carrying John F. Kennedy Jr, his wife, Carolyn, and his sister-in-law, Lauren Bessette, disappeared last night over the sea off Martha's Vineyard. Mr Kennedy was piloting the single-engine Piper Saratoga from New Jersey airport to a family wedding at Hyannis Port. He intended to stop off at Martha's Vineyard, but never arrived.

Today, a black bag with Lauren Bessette's name on it was washed ashore. An intensive air-to-sea search is currently in progress. (→ July 22)

JFK Jr and his wife, Carolyn, brought the Kennedy glamour to a new generation.

NEWCASTLE, THURSDAY 15
Judge forces girl to have transplant

A 15-year-old girl is today recovering in hospital after being forced to have a heart transplant against her will. A High Court judge ruled that the transplant should proceed even though the teenager, who cannot be named, had said she would rather die than have the operation. The judge agreed that there was a risk she might resent what had been done to her, but said this had to be matched against "the certainty of death".

BRITAIN, THURSDAY 15
M&S in trouble after sales slump

Marks & Spencer, an institution in high streets across Britain, today announced the sharpest fall in sales in its history, by 9 per cent year-on-year. Profits have also slumped to half their 1998 level. M&S's troubles are a symptom of the struggle facing established retailers as aggressive new competitors push down shop prices.

Unionist boycott undermines Ulster peace accord

This was supposed to be the week when the Northern Ireland peace process, enshrined in last year's Good Friday agreement, came to fruition. The parties in the Northern Ireland assembly were to nominate ministers to a power-sharing executive that would take over the government of the province. But when the assembly gathered in Belfast this morning, the 27 members of the Ulster Unionist Party and their leader, First Minister David Trimble, were missing.

Last night the Unionists rejected a final appeal by Prime Minister Tony Blair, who asked them not to close the door on "the best chance for peace in a generation". The party's executive stuck to its policy of "no guns, no government", refusing to take part in an executive with members of Sinn Fein until the IRA had begun to hand over its weapons.

The decision by the Unionists to boycott the assembly today led to a farcical session as the SDLP and Sinn Fein solemnly nominated members of an executive with no Unionist participation. However, Northern Ireland Secretary Mo Mowlam hastily issued a ruling that the executive could not be valid without at least three Unionists.

A rare moment of dignity on an otherwise chaotic day was provided by the deputy first minister, Seamus

Ulster Unionist David Trimble (left) and Seamus Mallon of the SDLP, men on opposite sides of the widening Northern Ireland divide.

Mallon of the SDLP. In a powerful speech, he told the assembly that he was resigning from a post rendered meaningless by the Unionists' action. He accused Unionist politicians of "dishonouring the agreement and insulting its principles". In direct contrast, Ian Paisley, the leader of the Democratic Unionist Party, welcomed the collapse of the agreement because, he said, it meant there were "no IRA men in government".

Clearly frustrated, Tony Blair and Irish Prime Minister Bertie Ahern announced that they were inviting George Mitchell, who negotiated last year's accord, to try to revive the peace process. (→ August 26)

Schumacher lucky to survive high-speed crash

German driver Michael Schumacher crashed his Ferrari at high speed into a tyre wall on the opening lap of today's British Grand Prix. It took rescue services 15 minutes to extricate him from the wreckage. His life was saved by improvements in racing car safety in recent years, allowing him to escape with two fractured bones in his right leg.

The race was won by McLaren's Scottish driver David Coulthard, with Ulsterman Eddie Irvine second. Former world champion Damon Hill was fifth. (→ July 25)

Schumacher's shattered Ferrari is lifted from the track after the accident that ended his championship hopes for this season.

President Kennedy's son buried at sea

Oxfordshire, 18
Six people are arrested after protesters severely damage an experimental crop of genetically modified oilseed rape at Model Farm near Watlington. (→ July 27)

Strasbourg, 19
The new 17-storey European parliament building opens. It cost £250 million. MEPs complain that it is dysfunctional and that much of its equipment, such as air-conditioning, does not work.

Washington, D.C., 19
In the latest round of a growing transatlantic trade war, the United States imposes punitive tariffs on European goods, including Danish ham and French foie gras, in retaliation for an EU ban on American beef treated with hormones.

Britain, 19
A report by the Institute for Fiscal Studies says that a third of all children in Britain are living in poverty.

Britain, 20
English tennis player Tim Henman announces his engagement to his girlfriend, TV producer Lucy Heald. The couple plan to marry in December.

Westminster, 20
The government announces that Britain is to be the first country to use a new anti-meningitis vaccine. Immunization will begin this autumn.

Britain, 20
The British Dental Association warns that wearing tongue studs can lead to serious infection and even death.

Massachusetts, 21
US Navy divers searching the sea bed off Martha's Vineyard locate the wreck of the aircraft in which John F. Kennedy Jr, his wife, and his sister-in-law died four days ago. (→ July 22)

Westminster, 21
Michael Ashcroft, Tory Party treasurer, issues a writ against *The Times*, which has been publishing allegations about his business affairs in Belize.

Cheshire, 22
In the hotly contested Eddisbury by-election, the Tories retain the seat with a slender majority of 1,606 votes.

DEATHS
July 23. King Hassan II of Morocco, ruler of his country for 38 years, dies of a heart attack, aged 70.

The USS Briscoe *embarks on a solemn mission to carry the ashes of John F. Kennedy Jr, his wife, and his sister-in-law for burial at sea.*

The Kennedy family today said farewell to another of its ill-fated sons. After a service on board a US Navy destroyer, the ashes of 38-year-old John F. Kennedy Jr, his wife, Carolyn, and her sister, Lauren Bessette, were scattered on the sea off Martha's Vineyard, Massachusetts, near where their aircraft crashed in the early hours of Saturday morning.

Born shortly after his father's victory in the 1960 US presidential elections, John F. Kennedy Jr was three days short of his third birthday when the president was assassinated. Once rated as America's most eligible bachelor, he had recently set up a magazine, *George*, which he edited with some success. His wife was a publicist for Calvin Klein.

Accident investigators say that it may be many months before the cause of the crash is established. However, it has emerged that Kennedy was an inexperienced pilot who was not qualified to fly using instruments. He was also recovering from an ankle injury, which could have made it more difficult to operate the plane's foot-pedal controls.

James Major has heart operation after honeymoon

James Major, son of the former prime minister, John Major, has had a heart pacemaker fitted at St Mary's Hospital, Paddington. The operation was carried out shortly after his return from his honeymoon.

Major, who is 24, married former game show hostess Emma Noble two months ago. He had apparently been aware of a heart problem for some time, but had put off the operation until the wedding was over.

British army investigates massacre of 14 unarmed Serb farmers

General Sir Michael Jackson, the commander of K-For, the Nato-led peacekeeping force in Kosovo, today promised to hunt down those responsible for the worst massacre in the province since the withdrawal of Serb forces almost two months ago.

The killings occurred yesterday evening. A British patrol found the bodies of 14 Serb farmers, including a teenage boy, in a field outside the village of Gracko. They had been killed while bringing in the harvest. All had been shot at close range. It is assumed that they were killed by ethnic Albanian guerrillas, although General Agim Ceku, the most powerful figure in the Kosovo Liberation Army (KLA), joined General Jackson in condemning the massacre.

British military police have begun an investigation into the deaths of the 14 men. However, the massacre has underlined the inability of K-For to stop ethnic Albanians terrorizing the Kosovan Serb minority. It is estimated that half the province's Serbs have now fled to Serbia.

LONDON, MONDAY 19
Top DJ shot in suspected rap feud

Radio One DJ Tim Westwood is in hospital under police guard after being shot yesterday evening while returning from a performance at an open-air concert in south London.

Westwood was sitting at traffic lights in Kennington when two men on a motorbike drew up alongside his car and opened fire. A bullet passed through Westwood's right arm. A passenger was also hit.

Westwood is a major figure in the world of rap and hip-hop – a black music environment where white DJs are rare. Police suspect he may have been targeted by gangsters who are involved in the rap music scene.

Cape Canaveral, Friday 23. Colonel Eileen Collins (far left) became the first woman to command a US space mission when the shuttle *Columbia* lifted off this morning. Colonel Collins described the mission as a "huge milestone" for women and "long overdue".

LONDON, MONDAY 19
Dallaglio back in England squad despite drug storm

After two months in the sporting wilderness, former England rugby captain Lawrence Dallaglio today joined a group of 40 players in fitness training for this autumn's rugby World Cup. Dallaglio's international career had seemed at an end two months ago when the *News of the World* alleged that he had admitted involvement with drugs.

The matter is still the subject of an independent inquiry, but England coach Clive Woodward has clearly decided to gamble on Dallaglio's name being cleared. (→ August 25)

CARNOUSTIE, SUNDAY 18
Unknown Scotsman wins Open after Frenchman flounders

Van de Velde up the creek at the last hole.

In one of the strangest endings to a major golf tournament ever seen, an unknown Scottish golfer today won the British Open championship.

At the start of the tournament at Carnoustie, 30-year-old Paul Lawrie was number 159 in the world golf rankings. His chance of glory arose when Frenchman Jean van de Velde, apparently certain of victory, made a series of disastrous errors at the last hole, eventually playing from the water in his bare feet. His collapse led to a play-off, which Lawrie won with some inspired shots.

It is the first time that the Open has been won by a Scottish golfer for 68 years. Holding the trophy, the astonished Lawrie said: "I can't believe it. I think I'm going to cry."

Aberdonian Paul Lawrie poses with his wife, Marian, their two sons, and a new piece of silverware for the mantelpiece.

S	M	T	W	T	F	S
				1	2	3
4	5	6	7	8	9	10
11	12	13	14	15	16	17
18	19	20	21	22	23	24
25	26	27	28	29	30	31

Spielberg, 25
Eddie Irvine wins the Austrian Grand Prix. He is now two points behind the leader, Mika Hakkinen, in the Formula One World Championship. (→ August 1)

Lord's, 25
New Zealand's cricketers beat England by nine wickets in the second Test of the current series. It is New Zealand's first Test win at Lord's. (→ August 24)

Britain, 27
Ofwat, the water industry regulator, announces new price limits that should reduce domestic water bills by an average of 14 per cent in the year 2000.

Old Bailey, 27
Great Western Trains is fined £1.5 million for breaches of health and safety laws that may have contributed to the 1997 Southall rail crash, in which seven people died. (→ September 20)

Westminster, 27
A House of Commons committee criticizes the government's handling of transport, and especially its failure to improve London Underground.

Britain, 28
Liam Donaldson, the government's chief medical officer, advises people to watch next month's total eclipse "on telly" to avoid possible eye damage. (→ August 11)

London, 28
An official report says that police were at fault in their handling of the riot in the City of London last month.

London, 28
Former Liverpool goalkeeper Bruce Grobbelaar wins a libel action against the *Sun* over allegations that he took bribes to lose football matches. He was cleared of criminal charges in 1997.

Scotland, 28
Scottish sprinter Dougie Walker is cleared of drug charges by a disciplinary panel. The athlete has been suspended since failing a drugs test last December.

Washington, D.C., 29
President Bill Clinton is fined over $90,000 (£55,000) by a federal judge for having denied under oath that he had sex with Monica Lewinsky.

The Moon, 31
Nasa scientists crash a space probe, *Lunar Prospector,* into a crater at the Moon's south pole, hoping that the impact will provide evidence of water there.

NORFOLK, TUESDAY 27
Lord Melchett jailed after GM crop protest

Lord Melchett is led away by police after leading a raid on a field of GM maize.

Lord Melchett, the head of the environmental group Greenpeace in Britain, was today refused bail and remanded in custody after being charged with damaging a field of genetically modified maize.

A former Labour minister, Lord Melchett led Greenpeace members in a dawn raid on the GM maize at Walnut Tree Farm, Norfolk, yesterday. By the time the police arrived, almost half the crop had been destroyed. It was one of seven authorized trial plantings of GM crops.

Lord Melchett said: "The British public … do not want these trials to go ahead." But the owner of the farm, William Brigham, denouncing the attack, said the issue was "whether we want democratic government or anarchy". (→ October 2)

WESTMINSTER, WEDNESDAY 28
The government reshuffle that never happened

For weeks the press has been awash with rumours of an imminent government reshuffle, with prominent cabinet ministers apparently set for a change. Mo Mowlam, it was said, was to leave her post as Northern Ireland secretary, Frank Dobson was to quit the ministry of health, and John Prescott would lose some of his extensive portfolio of jobs.

However, both Mowlam and Dobson publicly campaigned against reallocation, and their pleas have been heard. Today, Prime Minister Tony Blair did announce a reshuffle, but one affecting only the smaller players in his government.

The most notable changes are the departure of Tony Banks from the ministry of sport and Glenda Jackson from her post as London transport minister. Both MPs intend to seek nomination as Labour candidate for London's mayor. Banks will also lead the campaign to bring the 2006 football World Cup finals to England.

The newspapers are angry at being misled by behind-the-scenes briefings and may be less cooperative with the government's spin machine in the future. (→ October 11)

SWITZERLAND, TUESDAY 27
Flash flood sweeps away tourists in Swiss gorge

A photo of the ill-fated "canyoning" party taken just before the tragic accident.

Nineteen tourists were killed today when a flash flood struck a mountain gorge near Interlaken, Switzerland. Two other people are missing.

The dead were with a group of 45 young people who were "canyoning", an activity that involves swimming, abseiling, and rock climbing along the course of a river. A torrential storm filled the Saxet Ravine with a wall of water, sweeping the victims helplessly downstream into Lake Brienz.

It is believed that the majority of the dead were Australians and New Zealanders, but at least one Briton is among those who have died.

Killer of 12 says: "Hope this doesn't ruin your day"

Mark Barton, a 44-year-old stock trader, ran amok today in a business district in Atlanta, Georgia, shooting nine people dead and injuring 13 others. He had earlier used a claw hammer to bludgeon his wife and two children to death in their suburban apartment. Barton fled the scene of the office massacre, but killed himself five hours later after being tracked down by police.

Witnesses described Barton as calm and unemotional during the massacre. He entered two neighbouring trading offices, firing on traders and employees. He reportedly quipped: "I hope this doesn't ruin your trading day." There were suggestions that he may have been motivated by heavy losses in speculation on stocks.

According to police, Barton had been the prime suspect in the brutal murders of his former wife and his mother-in-law, who were hacked to death on a camping trip in 1993. However, there had been insufficient evidence for him to be charged.

Commenting on the number of random killings in the United States in recent months, Atlanta's mayor, Bill Campbell, said: "A cancer is eating at the heart of the country."

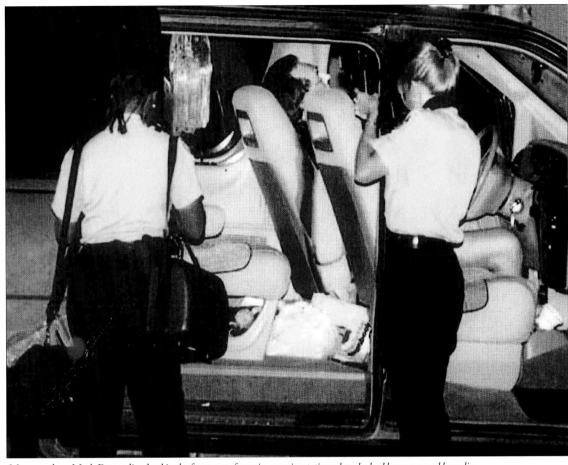

Mass murderer Mark Barton lies dead in the front seat of a car in a service station where he had been cornered by police.

Dublin, Monday 26. Snooker legend Alex Higgins today announced that he is taking legal action against two tobacco companies. He wants compensation for the throat cancer he is now fighting against. Higgins said he was "a living example of the dangers of smoking".

American cyclist conquers cancer and the Tour

Lance Armstrong, a 27-year-old cyclist from Texas, today won the Tour de France, one of the most gruelling sports events, only three years after recovering from cancer.

Doctors gave Armstrong a less than even chance of survival when he was found to have testicular cancer that had spread to his lungs and brain. He underwent prolonged chemotherapy and extensive surgery to defeat the disease.

Armstrong believes that his will to win has been strengthened by the experience of suffering. He told journalists: "We have all heard the saying 'what does not kill you makes you stronger', and that is exactly it."

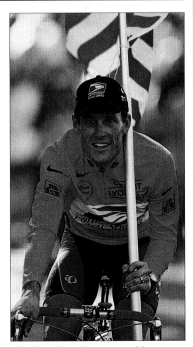

American Lance Armstrong celebrates victory in the 87th Tour de France.

S	M	T	W	T	F	S
1	2	3	4	5	6	7
8	9	10	11	12	13	14
15	16	17	18	19	20	21
22	23	24	25	26	27	28
29	30	31				

Europe, 1
The European Union ban on British beef exports, introduced during the BSE crisis, officially ends. (→ August 3)

Hockenheim, 1
Ferrari drivers Eddie Irvine and Mika Salo take first and second places, respectively, in this year's German Grand Prix. (→ August 15)

Britain, 2
According to the Halifax, house prices rose by 2 per cent last month, the sharpest rise since 1988.

Washington, D.C., 3
Arbitrators order the US government to pay $16 million for the 26-second 8-mm film of the assassination of President Kennedy taken by Abraham Zapruder.

Westminster, 3
The government announces that next year quarantine rules will be waived for pets that have been vaccinated against rabies and identified by a microchip tag.

Berlin, 3
The German government says that it will continue to block the import of British beef despite the lifting of the export ban by the EU two days ago. (→ October 15)

Brussels, 4
A meeting of Nato ambassadors confirms that British Defence Secretary George Robertson will be the alliance's new secretary-general. (→ August 24)

Westminster, 9
Charles Kennedy is elected as the Liberal Democrats' new leader. He wins 57 per cent of the vote in a straight contest with Simon Hughes. (→ August 15)

Moscow, 9
President Boris Yeltsin sacks his prime minister, Sergei Stepashin. His replacement is former spy Vladimir Putin.

London, 13
A High Court judge rules that Rolling Stones singer Mick Jagger and model Jerry Hall were never legally married.

DEATHS
August 4. Victor Mature, Hollywood idol of the 1940s and 1950s, dies aged 84.

August 8. Helen Rollason, popular BBC sports presenter, dies of cancer aged 43.

August 10. Jennifer Paterson, one of the Two Fat Ladies in BBC2's cookery series, dies of cancer aged 71.

WEST BENGAL, MONDAY 2
Hundreds feared dead in Indian rail catastrophe

More than 400 people are feared dead after two trains collided just before 2 a.m. at Gaisal in the Indian state of West Bengal. The Assam-to-Awadh Express ran head-on into the Delhi-bound Brahmaputra Mail. Both sleeper trains were travelling at around 50 mph.

Fifteen carriages were smashed into a mass of tangled metal and broken glass. Several of the carriages were also engulfed in flames. Rescuers and medical teams are still freeing injured people from the wreckage. An estimated 2,500 passengers were on the two trains.

Rio de Janeiro, Sunday 8. Today was the 36th anniversary of the Great Train Robbery as well as the 70th birthday of one of its perpetrators, Ronnie Biggs. The fugitive Biggs (above centre) celebrated the occasion with friends at his home in Rio.

LONDON, WEDNESDAY 4
Queen Mother enters her 100th year

The Queen Mother holds a balloon given to her by a birthday well-wisher in the crowd.

Queen Elizabeth the Queen Mother celebrated her 99th birthday today in remarkably sprightly style.

Emerging from her London home, Clarence House, she stood for 15 minutes as children filed up to hand her cards and gifts. She then spent another half an hour talking to people in the crowd that had gathered for the occasion. Only then did she resort to her golf buggy, which was suitably decorated with balloons.

PISA, SATURDAY 7
Blairs' Tuscan holiday is a PR disaster

Prime Minister Tony Blair held a holiday press conference today in an effort to stem a flood of damaging stories about what was intended to be a quiet family vacation.

The Blairs are staying at the Villa del Gombo on the Tuscan coast. The villa is owned by Tuscany's regional government and has been lent to the Blairs by regional president Vannino Chiti, a family friend. A luxurious holiday home, its ten rooms and seven bathrooms were recently renovated at a cost to Italian taxpayers of £380,000.

This might have passed without comment but for the decision by local police to close five miles of beach around the villa to ensure the prime minister's security and privacy. Local people were immediately up in arms, and were not fully placated even when Blair requested to have the beach reopened. The prime minister has also promised to make a donation to local children's hospitals in lieu of rent for the villa.

Blair told the press today: "I just want to have a good time with Cherie and the kids." But he knows better than most that a prime minister is never off duty. (→ August 16)

Christie drug-test shock

Linford Christie, 39, one of Britain's most respected athletes, has been suspended from competition after testing positive for a banned steroid, nandrolone, at an athletics meeting in Dortmund.

Protesting his innocence, Christie said that he had always opposed the use of banned substances, and it was ridiculous to imagine he would take them after retiring from top-level athletics. Nandrolone can appear in the body naturally. (→ September 6)

London, Monday 2. Desmond Lynam, the BBC's prestigious sports presenter, announced today that he is moving to ITV. It is another blow for the BBC's declining sports coverage.

Shearer sent off as league kicks off

The FA Carling Premiership season opened in acrimonious style today when England captain Alan Shearer, in his 100th match for Newcastle, was shown the red card as his team lost 0-1 to Aston Villa. Newcastle manager Ruud Gullit reacted heatedly, going onto the pitch to shout at referee Uriah Rennie at the end of the game. Both Shearer and his manager are under pressure after poor results last season. (→ August 28)

Total eclipse dampened by bad weather

Eclipse watchers, wearing the special viewers distributed as eye protection, peer for a sight of the event through the cloud and drizzle.

Television provided a safe and clearer alternative to viewing the eclipse directly.

From the North Atlantic Ocean to the Bay of Bengal, literally millions of people turned out today to witness the last total eclipse of the Sun in this millennium. In England, where south Devon and Cornwall lay within the band of totality, it was the first total eclipse since 1927. The next is not due in Britain until 2090.

The weather was not kind to English eclipse watchers, however. People who travelled to the West Country to enjoy the spectacle were met by overcast skies that allowed only partial glimpses of the phenomenon. But most declared even that an impressive experience.

Dire predictions of mass blindness as a result of staring at the Sun proved wide of the mark. Eye clinics received thousands of calls from worried people, but there were few reports of serious retinal damage.

The worst sufferers from the eclipse have been entrepreneurs who set up camp sites and open-air festivals in Cornwall. They have lost large sums as the number of visitors fell far short of expectations.

S	M	T	W	T	F	S
1	2	3	4	5	6	7
8	9	10	11	12	13	14
15	16	17	18	19	20	21
22	23	24	25	26	27	28
29	30	31				

Medinah Country Club, 15
American golfer Tiger Woods narrowly beats 19-year-old Spaniard Sergio Garcia to win the USPGA Championship.

Budapest, 15
Mika Hakkinen wins the Hungarian Grand Prix, closing to within two points of Eddie Irvine at the top of the drivers' championship. (→ August 29)

Siena, 16
Animal rights campaigners are outraged when Tony and Cherie Blair, on holiday in Tuscany, attend the Palio of Siena, a traditional race considered by some to be cruel to horses.

Newbury, 17
The Highways Agency announces that the Newbury bypass, completed ten months ago in the teeth of protests by green campaigners, is to close for repairs because its surface is cracking.

Birmingham, 18
Home Secretary Jack Straw stirs up controversy with outspoken comments about travellers. Speaking on BBC Radio West Midlands, he says that travellers who "masquerade as law-abiding Gypsies" are responsible for burglary, thieving, and defecating in doorways.

Westminster, 18
The government announces that there is to be a public inquiry into the 1989 *Marchioness* riverboat disaster on the Thames, in which 51 people died.

London, 19
Rail Regulator Tom Winsor says that Railtrack will be fined up to £42 million if it fails to cut delays to services caused by faulty track and signalling.

London, 20
Four men are found guilty of sabotaging floodlights during a football match between Charlton and Liverpool in 1997. They were working on behalf of a Far Eastern betting syndicate.

London, 21
Police investigating the murder of TV presenter Jill Dando say that the gun used in the killing was either homemade or adapted from a replica weapon.

DEATHS
August 15. Paddy Devlin, Northern Ireland politician, dies aged 74.

August 15. Sir Hugh Casson, architect of the 1951 Festival of Britain, dies aged 89.

Omagh, Sunday 15. The first anniversary of the bombing of the Northern Ireland town of Omagh, in which 29 people died, was marked today by a moving ceremony in the town centre. It was attended by more than 10,000 people, including relatives of the dead and some of the hundreds injured in the attack.

WESTMINSTER, SUNDAY 15
Liberal leader calls for drug rethink

Lib Dem leader Charles Kennedy (centre).

Elected as leader of the Liberal Democrats only last week, Charles Kennedy has already plunged head-first into controversy over drug abuse. In an interview published in the *Observer* today, Kennedy calls for a "mature and adult" debate on drugs and a royal commission to examine the failure of the current anti-drugs strategy. Both the Labour and Tory parties are officially opposed to any decriminalization of drugs.

NEW YORK, TUESDAY 17
Celebrities feel bad as Planet Hollywood is lost in space

The Planet Hollywood restaurant chain, backed by famous movie stars, has filed for bankruptcy. The company's celebrity shareholders include Sylvester Stallone, Bruce Willis, and Arnold Schwarzenegger.

Opened in New York in 1991, the first Planet Hollywood, with its neat formula of hamburger-and-fries served in a decor of movie memorabilia, proved so successful that soon there were 87 branches worldwide. But in recent years both the restaurant and the stars associated with it have come to look seriously dated.

Planet Hollywood's share price fell from $32 in 1996 to under $1 this year. Stallone apologized to investors, many of them fans, who lost money in the company. "It was a gamble on all people's behalf," he said. "Of course I feel very, very bad."

An idle doorman outside one of Planet Hollywood's 87 restaurants.

ISTANBUL, MONDAY 23

Turkish earthquake may have killed 40,000

Rescuers with sniffer dogs search for survivors in the rubble of a collapsed apartment building in an Istanbul suburb.

About a quarter of a million people have been left homeless by the earthquake.

Turkish authorities today ordered an end to the search for survivors amongst the rubble of towns and villages devastated by the earthquake that struck northwest Turkey last week. About 13,000 bodies have been found, but another 30,000 people are still missing. Ruined buildings are now being bulldozed in an attempt to prevent a mass outbreak of infectious diseases.

The earthquake, registering 7.5 on the Richter scale, struck at 3 o'clock on Tuesday morning, August 17. Along the densely populated northeast coast of the Sea of Marmara, from the suburbs of Istanbul to Izmit, Golcuk, and the coastal resort of Yalova, more than 100,000 buildings crashed to the ground within a minute. Moments later, a massive tidal wave swept ashore, smashing seafront cafes and hurling boats into shop fronts.

Across a large area of northern Turkey, bridges were destroyed and communications disrupted. There was also significant damage in the Turkish capital, Ankara, 200 miles east of Istanbul.

As people recovered from their initial shock, grief turned to anger, directed against property companies that had constructed shoddy concrete buildings that collapsed at the first tremor, and against the Turkish government, apparently incapable of organizing a relief effort. The struggle to find people trapped under rubble was led by foreign relief teams and Turkish volunteers.

Ordinary people scrabbled through the ruins with their bare hands trying to salvage what they could from their shattered homes.

S	M	T	W	T	F	S
1	2	3	4	5	6	7
8	9	10	11	12	13	14
15	16	17	18	19	20	21
22	23	24	25	26	27	28
29	30	31				

Westminster, 24
Defence Secretary George Robertson, recently appointed secretary-general of Nato, is given a peerage, becoming Lord Robertson of Port Ellen.

Westminster, 24
It is announced that individual hereditary peers will be allowed a maximum of 75 words to explain why they should be among the 92 hereditaries to retain their seats in the Lords. (→ October 26)

Seville, 25
At the World Athletics Championships, British athlete Colin Jackson wins a gold medal in the 100 m hurdles. Another Briton, Dean Macey, wins a silver medal in the decathlon.

Twickenham, 25
Former England rugby captain Lawrence Dallaglio is fined £15,000 by the Rugby Football Union over statements he made to a newspaper claiming that he had in the past been involved with illegal drugs.

Britain, 25
Rail Regulator Tom Winsor reveals that over a million complaints were made about train services last year.

Outer Space, 27
The last crew leaves Russia's 13-year-old *Mir* space station. *Mir* will splash down in the Pacific Ocean next spring.

Edinburgh, 27
According to a report in *The Scotsman*, the Serbs were able to shoot down a Stealth fighter in the first week of the Kosovo War because a spy at Nato headquarters betrayed its flight plan.

St James' Park, 28
Ruud Gullit resigns as Newcastle United manager, claiming he wants his "own private life back". (→ September 19)

Spa, 29
Scottish driver David Coulthard wins the Belgian Grand Prix ahead of his McLaren colleague, drivers' championship leader Mika Hakkinen. (→ September 26)

Moscow, 31
A bomb explodes in a shopping mall, injuring at least 29 people. Chechen terrorists are suspected of being behind the attack. (→ September 13)

France, 31
French farmers protesting at punitive American duties on Roquefort cheese and other products picket McDonald's restaurants throughout the country.

Brown rules out state cash for sheep farmers as prices plummet

Agriculture Minister Nick Brown, on a recent foray into sheep-farming country.

Prices for British lambs and ewes have now fallen so low that some farmers have taken to dumping the animals in protest. More than 300 sheep were abandoned at an RSPCA centre in Wales last week. But Agriculture Minister Nick Brown today ruled out state subsidy for sheep farmers. He said that the farmers were partly responsible for the crisis, as they had reacted to falling prices by breeding more lambs.

A farmers' spokesman said Brown was being "misleading", and blamed the crisis on health regulations and the strong pound. (→ September 21)

Call for memorial on anniversary of Diana's death

On the second anniversary of the car crash in which Diana, Princess of Wales, died, tributes were left by her most fervent admirers at the gates of Kensington Palace. The public display drew attention to the fact that the Diana Memorial Committee, set up after the tragedy, has still failed to establish a permanent focus for mourning. Followers of Diana today collected signatures for a petition demanding a memorial.

Meanwhile, sections of the report of the official inquiry into the fatal crash, to be released next week, have been leaked to the press. The report, by French Judge Herve Stephan, says that pursuing photographers did not hound the princess to her death, as had been alleged. Rather, the crash was caused by the chauffeur, Henri Paul, who was not qualified to drive a Mercedes. Paul was also drunk. The report adds that if Dodi Fayed and Diana had been wearing seat belts, they might have survived.

London, Monday 30. A record one million people flocked to watch the spectacular floats and listen to the steel bands at this year's Notting Hill Carnival over the Bank Holiday weekend. According to the police, it was the most crime-free carnival of the last decade, with just 43 arrests for minor offences.

Ceasefire not broken, says Mo

Secretary of State for Northern Ireland Mo Mowlam faced a barrage of criticism from Ulster Unionists today after ruling that the IRA ceasefire was still in place.

Mowlam described acts of violence carried out by the IRA in recent months, including the murder of Belfast taxi driver Charles Bennett, as "utterly deplorable". But she said that, although the IRA had "sailed close to the wind", the ceasefire had not broken down.

Mowlam's decision means that the controversial release of terrorist prisoners will continue. (→ October 11)

Secretary of State Mo Mowlam, seen by Ulster Unionists as soft on the IRA.

IRELAND, TUESDAY 31

Priest apologizes for "slut" slur

Catholic priest Seamus Duffy today apologized for a sermon in which he described one of Ireland's most popular athletes as a "common slut".

Champion long-distance runner Sonia O'Sullivan had a baby in July. She is in a long-term relationship, but is not married. Father Duffy took her as an example in an impassioned attack on the moral decline of Irish society. Today he said: "I am sorry if I hurt her and regret in particular the use of the word 'slut'."

East Timorese defy militias to vote for independence

Anti-independence militias bring violence to the streets of the East Timorese capital, Dili.

The population of East Timor today flocked to vote in a UN-organized referendum on independence from Indonesia. East Timor was annexed by Indonesia in 1975 after the territory's colonial rulers, the Portuguese, hurriedly withdrew. For more than two decades, Timorese resistance to Indonesian rule has been suppressed with extreme loss of life.

An estimated 95 per cent of the territory's 430,000 voters turned up at polling stations today, despite a systematic campaign of intimidation by pro-Indonesian militias in the run-up to the election. More than 100 people have been killed and an estimated 40,000 driven from their homes in recent violence.

Election day has proved largely peaceful, however. UN Secretary-General Kofi Annan said that voting had taken place in "a calm and dignified manner". People queued outside polling booths for hours, then cast their votes, and, as advised by the UN, left quietly for home.

The high turnout is widely regarded as certain to produce a substantial majority in favour of independence for East Timor. There are serious fears, however, that Indonesia and its supporters in East Timor will continue to resist independence by force, precipitating a further bloodbath. Calls have already been made for a UN peacekeeping force to be sent to the territory. At present, only the Indonesian army, which is widely regarded as being in league with the militias, is in place to maintain order. (→ September 20)

English Channel, Tuesday 24. The cruise liner *Norwegian Dream*, **with 2,400 people on board, had its bow wrecked when it collided with a container ship at the North Sea end of the English Channel today. The container ship caught fire, but no one was seriously injured.**

ENGLAND, TUESDAY 24

English cricketers ranked the worst in the world

The English are reluctantly coming to terms with the fact that they are at the bottom of the world league in a sport that they created: cricket.

Playing at the Oval on Sunday, the England team lost to New Zealand by eight wickets, giving the Kiwis a 2–1 victory in the four-match Test series – one match was drawn. It was a humiliating defeat, with the last seven England wickets being surrendered for a meagre 19 runs.

Before this series, New Zealand had been at the bottom of the Wisden World Championship table, an unofficial but widely accepted ranking of the nine Test-playing countries. Now, England have taken their place at the foot of the table for the first time. The future of England's recently appointed captain, Nasser Hussain, may well be in doubt.

S	M	T	W	T	F	S
			1	2	3	4
5	6	7	8	9	10	11
12	13	14	15	16	17	18
19	20	21	22	23	24	25
26	27	28	29	30		

Westminster, 5
In a newspaper interview, Prime Minister Tony Blair calls for "a new national moral purpose". He is particularly reacting to news reports last week that two 12-year-old girls are pregnant.

Britain, 6
A UK Athletics disciplinary panel clears athlete Linford Christie of a charge of taking a performance-enhancing drug.

Athens, 7
An earthquake shakes the Greek capital, killing at least 30 people.

City of London, 8
The Bank of England raises the base rate from 5 to 5.25 per cent, reversing a year-long fall in interest rates.

Northern Ireland, 9
In a controversial report on the Royal Ulster Constabulary (RUC), Chris Patten recommends changes including a new name – the Northern Ireland Police Service – a new oath to uphold human rights, and the removal of portraits of the Queen from police stations in Ulster.

Warsaw, 9
England's footballers draw 0-0 with Poland in a European Championship qualifier. England can now only reach playoffs for the championship if Poland lose to Sweden. (→ October 9)

London, 10
The first attempt to raise the world's largest Ferris wheel on the bank of the Thames fails ignominiously. The wheel is meant to be a centrepiece of London's millennium celebrations. (→ October 10)

Burma, 16
Rachel Goldwyn, 28, from Barnes, is sentenced to seven years in jail by a Burmese court for chaining herself to a lamppost and singing a protest song in front of a large crowd. (→ November 1)

London, 20
The Southall rail crash inquiry is told that driver Larry Harrison was seen with his feet on the dashboard of his cab before the accident. (→ October 5)

DEATHS
September 17. Frankie Vaughan, born Frank Abelson, romantic singer of the 1950s and 1960s, dies aged 71.

September 20. Raisa Gorbachev, wife of the former president of the Soviet Union, Mikhail Gorbachev, dies aged 67.

Peacekeepers go into East Timor

An Australian peacekeeper goes about his business of protecting the local population under the sullen gaze of Indonesian troops.

A UN peacekeeping force, commanded by Australian General Peter Cosgrove, is today in control of the East Timorese capital, Dili, ending three weeks of violence that shocked the international community.

In a UN-supervised referendum last month, nearly 80 per cent of East Timorese voted for independence from Indonesia. Despite warnings that anti-independence militias would react violently to a pro-independence vote, the UN had only an unarmed civilian mission in the territory. When the militias, backed by Indonesian troops, went on the rampage, the UN civilians were withdrawn for their own safety.

There was a long delay in sending a peacekeeping force because it had to wait for approval from the Indonesian government. By the time the first peacekeepers, including British Gurkhas, arrived yesterday, Dili was a ghost town, with street after street of burnt-out buildings. The UN estimates that nine-tenths of the population of East Timor have been driven from their homes, many herded across the border into Indonesian-controlled West Timor.

The peacekeepers' first tasks are to disarm the militias and distribute food to refugees. Then, it is hoped, East Timor will continue on the path to independence. (→ October 20)

Robson is back with a sackful of goals

Former England manager Bobby Robson will not forget his first home game as Newcastle United manager. Signed up, at the age of 66, to replace Ruud Gullit as manager of a club in crisis, he today saw his team win 8-0 against Sheffield Wednesday, with his troubled star striker, Alan Shearer, scoring five goals.

The result was all the more remarkable for being the club's first Premiership victory of the season. Robson's laconic comment was "Now we can begin to improve."

Bobby Robson acknowledges an enthusiastic welcome from the Newcastle United fans.

LONDON, WEDNESDAY 8
Portillo comes clean about his gay past

In an interview with *The Times*, former Tory minister Michael Portillo today revealed that he had "some homosexual experiences as a young person". He stressed that he was now happily married, and that he had spoken out to stop "vicious rumours" circulating about his sexuality.

Portillo lost his seat in the 1997 election, but is putting himself forward for the Kensington and Chelsea constituency following the death of its MP, Alan Clark. (→ November 2)

Saltwood Castle, Kent, Sunday 5. Tory MP Alan Clark died today, aged 71. A junior minister from 1983 to 1992, and a military historian, he became widely known for his *Diaries*, published in 1995. They painted a frank self-portrait of the author as a womanizer and eccentric.

BEXLEYHEATH, SATURDAY 11
Suburban granny named in spy revelations

Former Soviet spy Melita Norwood, aged 87, in the front garden of her suburban house.

An 87-year-old great-grandmother living in suburban Bexleyheath has been revealed as a spy who worked for the former Soviet Union.

Melita Norwood was an agent code named "Hola". From the 1930s to the 1950s, she passed the Soviets secrets from the metals research organization where she worked, some relevant to development of the atom bomb. In a statement today, Norwood said she had not done it for money, but to put Russia "on an equal footing with the West".

More spy revelations are expected, based on material provided by former KGB officer Vasili Mitrokhin, who defected in 1992. (→ October 21)

FRIDAY, THURSDAY 2
Storm as Edward knocks Britain

The Earl of Wessex, known in the United States as Edward Windsor, has caused outrage in Britain with remarks published in an American newspaper. Prince Edward told the *New York Times* that the American response to his ideas for television programmes had been "a breath of fresh air". Lauding the "greater openness" of the United States, he said the British "hate anyone who succeeds".

In an apology issued today, Prince Edward said that "offending the British public was the very last thing I would have wanted to do."

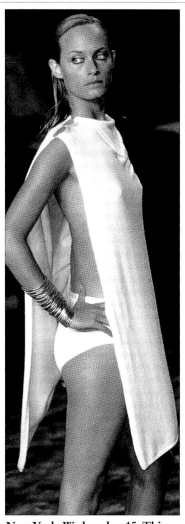

New York, Wednesday 15. This summer's New York fashion week was remarkable for the quantity of bare flesh that designers required their models to display on the catwalk.

MOSCOW, MONDAY 13
Chechen bombers spread terror in Moscow

The Russian capital, Moscow, is today in a state of shock after its second major terrorist bombing in five days. In the early hours of this morning a huge explosion demolished an eight-storey block of flats in the southern suburbs of the city. At least 73 people are known to have died, although the death toll could rise to over 100. An almost identical bombing killed 93 people in another Moscow apartment block last week.

In a special television broadcast, Russian President Boris Yeltsin said: "Terrorism has declared war on the Russian people." The authorities are convinced that the bombings are the work of Chechen separatists. A long-drawn-out conflict between Russia and Chechnya is still simmering. Russian forces are also currently engaged in a military campaign against separatists in Chechnya's neighbour, Dagestan. (→ October 1)

S	M	T	W	T	F	S
			1	2	3	4
5	6	7	8	9	10	11
12	13	14	15	16	17	18
19	20	21	22	23	24	25
26	27	28	29	30		

Westminster, 21
Agriculture Minister Nick Brown announces a £150 million aid package for livestock farmers and says that the ban on beef on the bone should be lifted by the end of the year.

Britain, 22
Tickets for the Millennium Dome go on sale at £20 each, or £57 for a family. The allocation for the opening day, January 1, is sold out within hours.

New York, 23
Doctors announce that an ovarian tissue transplant operation has been carried out at a New York hospital. Pioneered by a British scientist, Professor Roger Gosden, the technique could potentially be used to reverse the effects of the menopause.

Mars, 23
The *Mars Climate Orbiter*, a space probe intended to study Martian weather, crashes into the planet because of a navigational error. The error was due to confusion between metric and imperial units when inputting data.

Suffolk, 24
Police find the body of missing teenager Vicky Hall, abducted five days ago while returning from a Felixstowe nightclub to her home in Creeting St Peter.

Nürburgring, 26
English driver Johnny Herbert wins the European Grand Prix. (→ October 17)

South Africa, 27
Twenty-six British tourists and a local guide are killed when their coach crashes on a mountain road near Lydenburg.

Strasbourg, 27
The European Court of Human Rights rules that Britain's ban on homosexuals in the armed forces is unlawful. Four gays had taken their case to the European Court after being sacked from the forces.

Stockholm, 30
This year's Nobel Prize for Literature is awarded to German novelist Gunter Grass, author of *The Tin Drum*.

DEATHS
September 22. George C. Scott, American actor, famous for his performances in films such as *The Hustler*, *Dr Strangelove*, and *Patton*, dies aged 71.

September 22. Clive Jenkins, prominent trade union leader of the 1970s and 1980s, dies aged 73.

BOURNEMOUTH, TUESDAY 28

Blair calls for war on conservatism

In an inspirational keynote speech to the Labour Party conference at Bournemouth today, Prime Minister Tony Blair declared that the key political battle of the 21st century would be between "the forces of progress and the forces of conservatism". He pledged that he would free the "extraordinary talent of the British people" from obstruction by "conservatism of left or right".

Blair frequently struck a personal note. After listing some of the problems of modern Britain, including unemployment, underinvestment in schools and hospitals, and children living in poverty, he asked delegates: "Do you think I don't feel this, in every fibre of my being?"

He set his vision of a fair society against Old Labour egalitarianism: "Not equal incomes … but an equal chance of fulfilment, equal access to knowledge and opportunity."

Although short on precise policy commitments, the speech was well received by delegates. Opinion polls currently show Labour maintaining a commanding lead over the Tories.

The prime minister in inspirational mood addressing the party faithful in Bournemouth.

NEW YORK, WEDNESDAY 29

BritArt offends New York mayor

Protesters react to Mayor Giuliani's tough action over the BritArt Sensation show.

Rudy Giuliani, the mayor of New York City, has cut off funding from the Brooklyn Museum of Art because it is showing works by British artists that he regards as "sick and disgusting". Mayor Giuliani has especially objected to Turner Prize winner Chris Ofili's picture of the Virgin Mary decorated with elephant dung.

Leaders of New York's art world have written to the mayor expressing "profound regret" at his decision.

TAIWAN, TUESDAY 21

Taiwan is hit by monster earthquake

The island state of Taiwan has been hit by its most powerful earthquake for three decades, measuring 7.6 on the Richter scale.

The epicentre of the earthquake, which struck in the early hours of this morning, was at Nantou in central Taiwan, but there was also large-scale damage in the capital, Taipei. So far, more than 1,700 people are known to have died, 4,000 have been injured, and a further 3,000 are missing.

Observers have been impressed by the efficiency of the authorities' response to the disaster. President Lee Teng-hui visited Nantou by helicopter during the day.

This is the fourth major earthquake this year, following those in Colombia in January, Turkey in August, and Greece two weeks ago.

BOSTON, SUNDAY 26
"Disgusting scenes" as US wins Ryder Cup

The United States today staged a remarkable comeback to win golf's Ryder Cup. At the start of the day, Europe led by ten points to six, but the Americans won eight of the final 12 games to win by one point.

The victory was blemished, however, when American players and their families began leaping around the green in celebration while Jose Maria Olazabal waited to play a putt that could still have won Europe the cup. Europe's vice-captain, Sam Torrance, said these were "the most disgusting scenes I have ever seen on a golf course". America's Tom Lehmann admitted it was "not a good thing", but explained: "Sometimes you get carried away."

Unseemly rejoicing breaks out in the American camp after Justin Leonard sinks the tournament-winning putt.

LONDON, WEDNESDAY 22
Diana Ross in airport arrest row

Police release Diana Ross from custody.

Pop legend Diana Ross was today arrested at London's Heathrow airport after an acrimonious encounter with an airport security officer.

Ross, 55, reacted angrily when her breasts were allegedly touched by a female officer during a security check. She then boarded a Concorde en route to New York, but was taken off the plane by police and held for five hours, before being released with a caution. Describing it as the worst experience of her life, Ross said she felt "violated and humiliated".

JAPAN, THURSDAY 30
Nuclear accident "worst since Chernobyl"

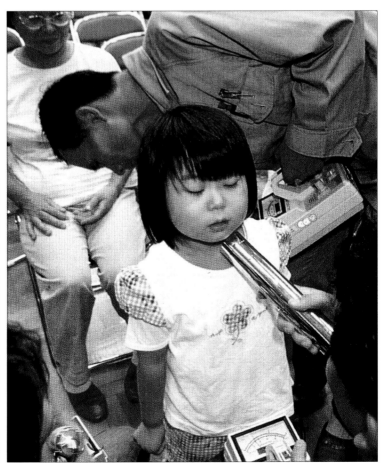

An explosion today seriously damaged the Tokaimura nuclear fuel plant, 100 miles northeast of the Japanese capital, Tokyo. The incident is being described as possibly the worst nuclear accident since the Chernobyl disaster in 1986.

About 300,000 people living in the densely populated area around the Tokaimura plant have been told to stay in their houses and seal all windows. At least 14 workers at the plant have been airlifted to hospital after exposure to radiation levels 15,000 times greater than normal. Two workers were showing classic signs of radiation sickness, including diarrhoea and fever.

Although the exact cause of the explosion is not yet known, first reports suggest that the accident happened when too much uranium was put in a tank of nitric acid, starting a nuclear fission chain reaction. The resulting explosion blew a hole in the roof of the building, releasing radiation into the atmosphere.

Speaking on behalf of the Japanese government, Chief Cabinet Secretary Hiromu Nonaka described the Tokaimura accident as "an unprecedented event in the history of nuclear power in this country".

A Japanese child is checked for radioactivity with a Geiger counter after the nuclear accident.

S	M	T	W	T	F	S
					1	2
3	4	5	6	7	8	9
10	11	12	13	14	15	16
17	18	19	20	21	22	23
24	25	26	27	28	29	30
31						

San Diego, 1
British nanny Manjit Kaur Basuta is sentenced to 25 years in jail after being found guilty of shaking to death a 13-month-old baby in her care.

London, 1
Lord Archer is selected as Conservative candidate for mayor of London, defeating Steven Norris by 15,716 votes to 6,350.

Chechnya, 1
Russian ground forces advance into Chechnya after nine days of airstrikes against the breakaway republic.

London, 2
Britain's top medical journal, *The Lancet*, announces that it is to publish research by Dr Arpad Pusztai suggesting that GM foods harmed rats. The research had been spurned by the scientific establishment.

Austria, 3
The far-right Freedom Party, led by Jörg Haider, wins 27 per cent of the votes in the country's general election.

Ibrox, 5
Scotland beat Bosnia-Herzegovina 1-0 to qualify for the play-offs for the European Championship finals. (→ October 13)

Preston, 5
The trial of GP Harold Shipman opens at Preston Crown Court. Shipman is charged with killing 15 women patients.

India, 7
The National Democratic Alliance, led by Atal Bihari Vajpayee, wins a clear majority in India's general election.

London, 8
A magistrate rules that General Augusto Pinochet can be extradited to Spain. The final decision on extradition now lies with Home Secretary Jack Straw.

Stockholm, 9
Sweden's footballers beat Poland 2-0, allowing England to qualify for the play-offs for the European Championship finals. (→ October 13)

Old Trafford, 9
In the climax to the rugby league season, St Helens win the JJB Super League Grand Final, defeating Bradford 8-6.

DEATHS
October 3. Akio Morita, the Japanese businessman responsible for developing the Sony Walkman, dies aged 78.

BLACKPOOL, WEDNESDAY 6

Tory civil war over Europe mars party conference

Conservative leader William Hague wanted to use this year's party conference to establish "common-sense" policies as the basis for victory in the next general election. But instead, the Tories are once more presenting a spectacle of disunity because of their apparently irresolvable differences over Europe.

Former prime minister Baroness Thatcher outraged pro-European Tories with an off-the-cuff remark at a fringe meeting yesterday. She told delegates: "In my lifetime, all the problems have come from mainland Europe, and all the solutions have come from the English-speaking nations across the world."

From the other side of the party, pro-European former deputy prime minister Michael Heseltine earlier launched a swingeing attack on Hague's European policy, describing it as "incalculable folly". Hague has adopted an increasingly hard line on Europe recently, in particular pledging to keep Britain out of European monetary union during the first term of a new Tory government.

Heseltine and former Tory chancellor of the exchequer Kenneth Clarke have agreed to join Prime Minister Tony Blair and prominent Liberal Democrats to launch a "Britain in Europe" pressure group later in the month. (→ October 14)

Cardiff, Friday 1. The fourth rugby union World Cup got under way this afternoon with an inventive display of Welsh pageantry at the new Millennium Stadium in Cardiff. A crowd of 70,000 then saw Wales beat Argentina 23-18 in a scrappy and sometimes violent match. Twenty teams are competing for the cup. (→ October 15)

CARDIFF, FRIDAY 1

Zavaroni dies after anorexia surgery

Lena Zavaroni: she could not cope with the transition from child star to adult performer.

Former child singing star Lena Zavaroni died today aged 35, two weeks after undergoing major brain surgery in a bid to cure her of the eating disorder anorexia nervosa.

Zavaroni was "discovered" at the age of ten by the ITV talent show *Opportunity Knocks*. For several years she was a highly successful singer, but by her late teens she had disappeared from public view. Her final years were spent living on benefit in a one-bedroom council flat.

Her anorexia was first diagnosed when she was 13. At the time of her death she weighed under four stone.

OTTAWA, FRIDAY 8

Clinton says sorry after "Irish drunks" quip

Expressing his frustration at the lack of progress towards peace in Ulster, President Bill Clinton today compared the people of Northern Ireland to "a couple of drunks" trying to leave a bar. "When they get to the swing door," he said, "they turn right round and go back in."

The remarks, made on a trip to Ottawa, Canada, caused an outcry. The president swiftly apologized for "a metaphor that was inappropriate".

LONDON, TUESDAY 5

Carnage as commuter trains collide in rush-hour catastrophe

The wreckage of the two commuter trains at Ladbroke Grove: the precarious position of the carriages made rescue work slow and perilous.

More than 50 people are feared dead after a head-on collision between two commuter trains at Ladbroke Grove, west London, at 8.11 a.m. today. A Thames Trains turbo that had just left Paddington crossed into the path of a First Great Western express. The inbound 6.03 from Cheltenham was travelling at high speed with some 500 people on board.

The devastation caused by the impact was compounded by fireballs that engulfed parts of the wreckage. Dazed and bloodied survivors clambered out of broken windows. Many had suffered horrific burns.

Emergency services were swiftly on the scene, ferrying the injured to hospital. As they searched for survivors, rescue workers could hear the sound of mobile phones ringing in the wreckage as relatives or friends tried to contact those who they knew had been intending to travel on one of the trains.

Transport Secretary John Prescott (third from the left) visits the scene of the accident.

The estimated number of dead rose through the day. By nightfall, 26 bodies had been retrieved, but police estimated that the final death toll could be between 50 and 100.

Accident investigators say the turbo went through a red light at signal 109. The signal had been the subject of complaints from drivers, who said it was too hard to see. (→ October 6)

LONDON, WEDNESDAY 6

"At least 70 dead" as grim search for bodies goes on

Police announced today that 70 people believed to have been on the Paddington crash trains are missing presumed dead. Most of the dead are thought to have been incinerated in carriage H, the coach, gutted by fire, which was at the front of the express. Searchers have still not been able to enter the carriage. Few bodies have yet been identified, and uncertainty is worsening the agony of relatives of the missing. (→ October 8)

The painstaking search for bodies was a harrowing experience for rescue workers.

BRITAIN, FRIDAY 8

Rail safety shake-up in wake of death crash

Railtrack, the company responsible for track and signals, has today been ordered to make immediate improvements to 22 signals that, like signal 109 outside Paddington, have been repeatedly passed at red. The government has, however, refused to endorse allegations that Railtrack has put profits before safety.

Transport Secretary John Prescott has promised that rail safety will be upgraded regardless of expense. This suggests that the government will back Automatic Train Protection, a system previously blocked because of its high cost. (→ October 10)

S	M	T	W	T	F	S
					1	2
3	4	5	6	7	8	9
10	11	12	13	14	15	16
17	18	19	20	21	22	23
24	25	26	27	28	29	30
31						

United States, 11
Colt, the world's most famous gunmaker, announces that it is to stop production of handguns. The company is facing civil lawsuits brought by the relatives of victims shot by its weapons.

New York, 12
United Nations experts estimate that the world's population has reached six billion.

Paris, 13
Under a new French law, unmarried cohabiting couples, whether heterosexual or homosexual, can enjoy the same rights as married couples if they officially register their relationship.

Germany, 13
Held in Aachen, the draw for the play-offs for next year's football European Championship finals pits England against traditional rivals Scotland. (→ October 18)

Westminster, 13
The House of Lords rejects parts of the government's welfare reform legislation, including cuts in disability benefit.

Old Bailey, 13
Stalker Anthony Diedrick is found guilty of the 1994 murder of Dr Joan Francisco. The conviction follows a long struggle by Dr Francisco's family, who eventually forced the police to re-examine the evidence against Diedrick.

London, 14
Prime Minister Tony Blair, former Tory ministers Michael Heseltine and Kenneth Clarke, and Liberal Democrat leader Charles Kennedy launch a pro-European "Britain in Europe" campaign.

Helsinki, 15
At a European Union summit in Finland, Tony Blair threatens the French with legal action if they continue to ban British beef. (→ October 23)

Stockholm, 16
This year's Nobel Peace Prize is awarded to the French humanitarian organization Médecins Sans Frontières.

Britain, 16
Twenty-six players are sent off in the English and Scottish football leagues, a record for red cards in a single day.

DEATHS
October 14. Julius Nyerere, African statesman, former president of Tanzania, dies in London aged 77.

Rail crash death toll drops

Police today radically reduced their estimate of the death toll in the Paddington rail disaster, after investigators searching carriage H, the front coach of the express involved, found only one body. There had been fears that as many as 50 people might have been incinerated in the carriage.

So far 30 bodies have been found in the wreckage of the two trains. Police said that estimates of the death toll had been inflated by bogus calls to missing-person hotlines.

Relatives of those known to have died in the crash held an open-air memorial service near the scene of the accident this afternoon.

Two-year-olds "too fat", say experts

In an article published in today's *British Medical Journal*, nutritionists argue that one in five toddlers is in need of a programme of diet and exercise to counter obesity.

The nutritionists, from Bristol and Glasgow universities, say that children as young as two years old are suffering from an overdose of junk food and passive television viewing. In effect, many of the nation's children are turning into "teletubbies".

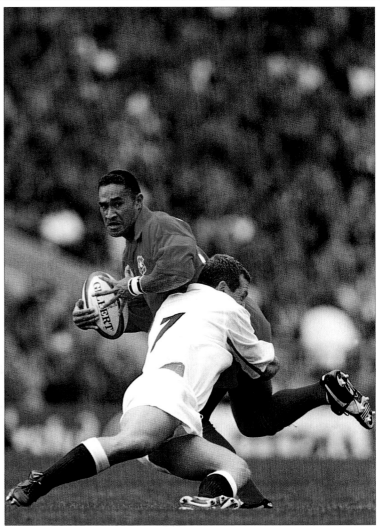

Twickenham, Friday 15. In the rugby World Cup, England beat Tonga 101–10, their highest score in World Cup finals – here, Hill tackles Tiueti. The first round of the tournament has been marred by the imbalance between the major and minor sides. (→ October 20)

London's millennium Ferris wheel goes up at last

The Ferris wheel alongside the Thames, still awaiting the cabins that will hold its passengers.

After an embarrassing false start four weeks ago, contractors today succeeded in raising the world's largest Ferris wheel, British Airways London Eye, near to the vertical.

The giant wheel is on the south bank of the Thames. Standing 135 m tall, three times as high as Tower Bridge, it is by far the most prominent structure being built for the millennium celebrations.

The first attempt to raise the wheel failed dismally, but today there was applause from spectators as it inched slowly skyward. The contractors now have to race to make the wheel operational by the start of the new millennium. (→ October 25)

Mandelson is back in place of Mo

Prime Minister Tony Blair acted decisively today to reshape his government, bringing his close ally Peter Mandelson back from ten months of political exile to replace Mo Mowlam in the demanding post of Northern Ireland secretary.

The reshuffle was triggered by the departure of Health Secretary Frank Dobson, who is leaving to stand for London mayor, and Defence Secretary Lord Robertson, recently appointed Nato secretary-general. They are replaced by Alan Milburn and Geoff Hoon respectively.

The prime minister apparently felt that, for all her success as Northern Ireland secretary, Mo Mowlam was no longer the person most likely to revitalize the stalled peace process. She now takes Jack Cunningham's place as cabinet office minister, the so-called "enforcer" responsible for co-ordinating government policies.

Mandelson's appointment in place of Mowlam was welcomed by Ulster

Peter Mandelson, pleased to be back after ten months in the political wilderness.

Unionist spokesman Ken Maginnis, who said it was "time we had a hard head rather than a hasty heart". But Tory chairman Michael Ancram said that Mandelson's return to cabinet was premature, especially as he had "shown not an ounce of remorse" for the undisclosed loan from Geoffrey Robinson that brought him into disgrace last December.

General takes power in Pakistan coup

The democratically elected prime minister of Pakistan, Nawaz Sharif, is under arrest this evening after a military coup. Sharif was surrounded by armed soldiers as he was about to address the nation on state television.

The leader of the coup is General Pervez Musharraf, who had just been sacked by the prime minister from his post as army chief of staff. The two men fell out during the summer when Sharif refused to back military action against India on the disputed Kashmir border.

Justifying the coup, the general accused Sharif of following "self-serving policies that rocked the very foundation of Pakistan". In the capital, Islamabad, a crowd on the streets shouted "Long live the army". The British and American governments, however, have called for a swift return to democracy. (→ October 19)

Ferrari shocked by technical knock-out

In a remarkable sequence of events today, the Ferrari Formula One team took first and second places in the Malaysian Grand Prix, only to be disqualified on a technicality. If the decision stands, Ferrari's main rival, McLaren, will have won the drivers' and constructors' championships.

In his first race since his accident in the British Grand Prix, Ferrari driver Michael Schumacher had shepherded his Ulster colleague, Eddie Irvine, to victory. The result put Irvine ahead of McLaren's Mika Hakkinen in the drivers' table and Ferrari at the top of the constructors' table going into the final race of the season, the Japanese Grand Prix.

But a post-race inspection found that the barge boards on the side of the Ferrari cars were 10 mm smaller than is allowed under Formula One's complex technical regulations. Hakkinen has been declared champion, pending an appeal. (→ October 23)

Ferrari drivers Eddie Irvine and Michael Schumacher enjoy their brief moment of victory, before being disqualified by the stewards.

S	M	T	W	T	F	S
					1	2
3	4	5	6	7	8	9
10	11	12	13	14	15	16
17	18	19	20	21	22	23
24	25	26	27	28	29	30
31						

London, 19
A meeting of Commonwealth foreign ministers calls on Pakistan's new military government to return the country to democracy and bans Pakistan from any involvement in the Commonwealth.

Britain, 20
In the wake of the Paddington rail crash, Railtrack's commercial director, Richard Middleton, tells a Radio 4 interviewer that it is "time for the hysteria around rail safety to be calmed down".

Lens, 20
Ireland are knocked out of the rugby World Cup, losing 24-28 to Argentina in the play-off round. (→ October 23)

Indonesia, 20
Demonstrators battle with police in the Indonesian capital, Jakarta, after the national assembly fails to choose the country's most popular politician, Megawati Sukarnoputri, as president. Instead, the new president is Muslim leader Abdurrahman Wahid.

Chechnya, 20
More than 40 people are killed when five missiles hit the Chechen capital, Grozny. Russia, which is engaged in military action against Chechnya, denies carrying out the attack. (→ November 3)

London, 21
Addressing a head teachers' conference, Prime Minister Tony Blair calls for an end to the "culture of excuses" in schools, which "tolerates low ambitions … and treats poverty as an excuse for failure".

Westminster, 21
Home Secretary Jack Straw says that 87-year-old Melita Norwood, who spied for the Soviet Union, may face prosecution. Possible legal action against four other spies named in recent revelations is also being considered.

Cardiff, 23
Wales are knocked out of the rugby World Cup, losing 9-24 to Australia in the quarter finals. (→ October 24)

Paris, 23
An independent panel of judges reinstates Ferrari drivers Eddie Irvine and Michael Schumacher as first and second in the Malaysian Grand Prix. Stewards had disqualified the two drivers because their cars infringed technical regulations, but the judges rule that the cars were within permitted tolerances. (→ October 31)

Food war looms as French keep ban on British beef

Britain and France are locked in a potentially explosive confrontation over food imports. The crisis began when the French government announced that it intended to maintain its ban on the import of British beef, despite the decision of the European Union in August that British beef was now safe and exports could be resumed.

French intransigence on the issue has led to demonstrations by British farmers that have won increasing support from the British press and public. Newspapers have called for a boycott of French goods, and supermarkets have joined in with the selective removal of French produce from their shelves. This week, Asda withdrew French baguettes and brie, Budgens banned French apples and pears, and Tesco cancelled an order for mistletoe worth £2 million.

Animosities have been further fuelled by the revelation that the French have for years been feeding farm animals with sewage. A report issued by the European Commission yesterday described this procedure as "unacceptable".

British Agriculture Minister Nick Brown has announced that he is

British farmers demonstrated their anger at the continuing import of French farm produce.

personally boycotting French goods, but the government has ruled out a formal ban on French imports, which would be illegal under EU regulations. Prime Minister Tony Blair has threatened to take the case to the European Court, but he knows that such legal action could take years to reach a conclusion.

A group of scientists is meeting in Brussels tomorrow to examine evidence produced by the French to justify continuing their ban on British beef. (→ October 29)

Wembley ticket chaos as big match draws near

Next month's confrontation between England and Scotland in the play-offs for the European Championship finals has already caused an outbreak of football fever north and south of the border. When the 36,000 tickets allocated to England fans for the home leg of the two-match contest became available for telephone booking today, there were over a million calls to the Wembley hotline. At one point, Wembley telephone exchange broke down completely under the pressure of callers.

Scots were outraged to discover that ticket sellers had been instructed to refuse to sell seats to callers with Scottish names, accents, or addresses. They were told to buy tickets from the Scottish FA. (→ November 13)

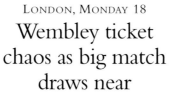

Detroit, Saturday 23. In round five of a world featherweight title bout tonight, British boxer Naseem Hamed body-slammed his Mexican opponent, Cesar Soto, to the canvas like a wrestler. Despite protests, Hamed was not disqualified. He went on to win the bout on points.

LONDON, FRIDAY 22

Chinese president's visit dogged by protests

The Queen and the Duke of Edinburgh greet Chinese President Jiang Zemin and his wife at the start of the controversial state visit.

Chinese President Jiang Zemin today completed a four-day state visit to Britain, the first ever by a Chinese communist leader.

The visit was intended to cement a growing economic relationship between the two countries, but protesters ensured that the issues of human rights violations in China and China's occupation of Tibet were brought to public attention.

The police have been criticized in the British press for their sometimes heavy-handed treatment of demonstrators, who were mostly kept well away from the Chinese visitors. But members of the Chinese delegation complained that not enough had been done to control the protesters, whom they described as "those fighting for the inglorious cause of imperialism and colonialism".

The fact that Prince Charles yesterday failed to turn up at a banquet at the Chinese embassy attended by the Queen has been widely interpreted as a deliberate snub to the communist leader. However, a Buckingham Palace spokesman pointed out that the prince had attended a banquet with President Jiang only two days earlier.

SIBERIA, MONDAY 18

Expedition retrieves entire frozen mammoth

The deep-frozen body of a woolly mammoth that died around 23,000 years ago has been dug out of the icy wasteland of northern Siberia. It is the first complete specimen of the extinct mammal to be found.

The mammoth's tusks were spotted by a Siberian family, the Zharkovs, two years ago. A team led by French explorer Bernard Buigues travelled to the site this year and identified the shape of the animal's body under the frozen ground.

This week, the permafrost enclosing the mammoth was excavated and carried by helicopter to an ice cave near the Siberian town of Khatanga. There it will be carefully defrosted using hairdryers.

Scientists say it may be possible to use the mammoth's DNA to create a living mammoth clone, using a cow elephant as surrogate mother.

Members of the expedition that excavated the mammoth pose behind its massive tusks.

London, Tuesday 19. Exhibits in the Tate's show of works shortlisted for this year's Turner Prize include Tracey Emin's *My Bed*. Strewn beside the bed are vodka bottles, contraceptives, and cigarette packets. (→ October 24)

Monroe memorabilia fetch millions at auction

An auction of former possessions of screen goddess Marilyn Monroe has elicited frantic bidding from around the world over the last two days.

The high-spot of the auction was the $1.15 million (£700,000) paid for the pink sequined dress that Monroe wore when she sang "Happy Birthday" to President Kennedy in 1962. A platinum eternity ring given to Monroe by her second husband, baseball player Joe DiMaggio, fetched $772,500 (£470,000).

The memorabilia, auctioned by Christie's at the Rockefeller Center in New York, were objects inherited by the widow of Monroe's former acting coach, Lee Strasberg.

Telephone bids are taken during the two-day auction of Marilyn Monroe's possessions.

S	M	T	W	T	F	S
					1	2
3	4	5	6	7	8	9
10	11	12	13	14	15	16
17	18	19	20	21	22	23
24	25	26	27	28	29	30
31						

Paris and Edinburgh, 24
England and Scotland are knocked out of the rugby World Cup. England lose 21-44 to South Africa at the Stade de France and Scotland go down 18-30 to New Zealand at Murrayfield. (→ October 31)

London, 24
At the Tate Gallery, Chinese performance artists Jian Jun Xi and Yuan Cai stage a pillow fight on Tracey Emin's Turner Prize shortlist exhibit *My Bed*. They say their action is intended as a protest against "institutionalized art".

London, 25
South African author J.M. Coetzee wins the Booker Prize for his novel *Disgrace*. He is the first novelist to win the annual prize twice – his previous success was with *Life and Times of Michael K* in 1983.

Westminster, 25
After a "rail safety summit" called by the government to consider the lessons of the Paddington rail crash, Transport Secretary John Prescott announces new standards for driver training and a hotline for drivers to report safety concerns.

London, 26
As Michael Portillo campaigns to be adopted as Tory candidate for Kensington and Chelsea, he is heckled by gays angered by the conflict between his admission of a homosexual past and his failure to back pro-gay legislation. (→ November 2)

Westminster, 26
The House of Lords passes the reform bill that will expel most hereditary peers from Parliament. The debate is marked by a protest by the Earl of Burford, who calls the bill "treason". (→ November 5)

Yerevan, 28
Terrorists, under siege in the Armenian parliament building after killing the prime minister, give themselves up.

London, 28
Arsenal's French international Patrick Vieira is fined a record £45,000 by the FA and banned for six matches. During a game between Arsenal and West Ham, Vieira reacted to being red-carded by spitting at an opposition player and swearing at a police officer.

Brussels, 29
A panel of scientists rules unanimously that France has no grounds for keeping its ban on British beef. (→ November 2)

Suzuka, Sunday 31. Finnish driver Mika Hakkinen won the Japanese Grand Prix today to become Formula One drivers' champion for the second consecutive year. But his team, McLaren-Mercedes, failed to take the constructors' title, which went instead to Ferrari.

Bold French rout the All Blacks

In what many believe to have been the finest match in rugby World Cup history, France beat the favourites New Zealand 43-31 today to go through to the final. The French scored 33 points in an explosive 30-minute period of the second half after falling 14 points behind the apparently invincible All Blacks.

France's opponents in the final will be Australia, who beat South Africa 22-21 after extra time in the other semifinal. (→ November 6)

Models' eggs up for sale on the Net

In a move that has outraged groups working to cope with infertility, an American website has put eggs donated by attractive models up for auction. Bids of up to $150,000 (£90,000) are being invited, presumably from wealthy men obsessed with having beautiful offspring.

A spokesman for the American Society for Reproductive Medicine described the scheme as distasteful and unethical. But the owner of the site, Ron Harris, said it would give men "the chance to have their genes combined with the most beautiful and genetically advanced women".

Golf champion dies in mystery crash

Prominent American golfer Payne Stewart was killed today when his Learjet crashed after flying out of control across the United States for over four hours. Four other people on board the aircraft also died.

Stewart and his companions took off from Orlando, Florida, at 9 a.m., intending to fly to Dallas, Texas. Half an hour into their flight, however, they stopped responding to air traffic control and veered off course, heading northwest across the United States. The aircraft was tracked by US fighter aircraft, ready to shoot it down if it seemed likely to crash in a built-up area. However, it eventually plummeted into a marshy field near Mina, South Dakota.

Accident investigators are pursuing the theory that the aircraft's cabin suffered a catastrophic drop in pressure at high altitude, killing those inside within seconds, but leaving the aircraft sufficiently undamaged to fly on until its fuel ran out.

Stewart was 42 years old. He was an immensely popular figure in the United States, noted for his sense of humour and infectious enthusiasm as well as for his golfing skills. He is the current US Open champion and was a member of this year's victorious US Ryder Cup team.

Payne Stewart was noted for his eccentric dress, wearing plus-twos and a tam-o'-shanter hat.

Prime minister shot in parliament massacre

Five gunmen opened fire in the parliament chamber of the former Soviet republic of Armenia today. Armenia's prime minister, Vazgen Sarkisyan, was shot dead, along with at least three of his colleagues. The gunmen are holding 50 people hostage in the building, which has been surrounded by security forces.

The attack began at 5.15 p.m. The five men walked into the building carrying weapons concealed under long overcoats. Entering the chamber, they shouted that they were launching a coup and opened fire. Television cameras continued to film as deputies scrambled for cover.

The motive behind the attack seems to be frustration at the dire state of Armenia's economy. Nairi Unanyan, one of the gunmen, said: "We do not have any demands, we simply want the people to live well."

The United States is currently trying to broker a peace deal between Armenia and Azerbaijan. The two countries have been in conflict over the disputed enclave of Nagorno-Karabakh. There are fears that today's killings may block progress in the peace negotiations. (→ October 28)

Britain, Sunday 24. Bobby Willis (right), the husband and business manager of show business personality Cilla Black (left), died yesterday aged 57. The couple met as working-class teenagers in Liverpool in the early 1960s. They married in 1969 and had three children.

Protesters take to the London Eye

A group of Green protesters climbed to the top of the newly erected London Eye Ferris wheel today. They were demonstrating against the building of dams in the Narmada Valley in India and in the Spanish Basque country.

Nine protesters originally occupied the wheel, unfurling banners. Seven of them came down voluntarily, but two, believed to be Basques, remained at the top of the wheel. Police officers with special training in climbing were sent up to negotiate with them, but they said they had supplies to stay aloft for two days.

A spokesman for the protesters said that the wheel was "a good example of the waste of money that Western society is involved in". The wheel cost £20 million to build.

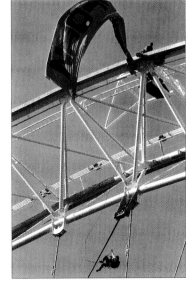

Protesters and police climbed on the wheel.

S M T W T F S

	1	2	3	4	5	6
7	8	9	10	11	12	13
14	15	16	17	18	19	20
21	22	23	24	25	26	27
28	29	30				

Rangoon, 1
Rachel Goldwyn, the British woman sentenced to seven years' imprisonment for singing a protest song, is released by the Burmese after seven weeks in jail.

London, 2
Former Tory minister Michael Portillo is adopted as the party's candidate for the safe seat of Kensington and Chelsea.

Britain, 2
The chief inspector of prisons, Sir David Ramsbotham, apologizes for having said that the child killers of toddler James Bulger should be released at the age of 18.

Brussels, 2
Despite the verdict of a panel of scientists last week that British beef is safe, Britain accepts French requests for further safety measures. (→ November 16)

Moscow, 3
Russia says it intends the total conquest of the breakaway republic of Chechnya. Russian air and artillery attacks have made 300,000 Chechens flee their homes.

Westminster, 5
The House of Lords selects the 75 hereditary peers who will keep their seats until a new second chamber is devised.

Westminster, 9
In his pre-budget report, Chancellor of the Exchequer Gordon Brown announces free television licences for people over 75.

Bristol, 12
Former rock star Gary Glitter is jailed for four months for downloading child pornography from the Internet.

Belfast, 15
Hopes rise for a successful end to the review of the Good Friday peace deal, chaired by American mediator George Mitchell, as Sinn Fein accepts that weapons decommissioning is "an essential part of the peace process".

United States, 16
A tape retrieved from the EgyptAir Boeing that crashed last week shows that a crew member said a Muslim prayer just before the plane went into free fall.

Brussels, 16
The European Commission begins legal proceedings against France over its refusal to lift a ban on British beef imports.

DEATHS
November 4. Malcolm Marshall, West Indian fast bowler, dies of cancer aged 41.

Scholes silences the Hampden roar

Manchester United midfielder Paul Scholes heads England's second goal as Scotland's defence fails to cope with a cross from David Beckham.

Billed in some newspapers as "the match of the century", England's encounter with Scotland in the first leg of their play-off for the European Championship finals next year fell well short of fulfilling the hype.

England were given a torrid reception by the 50,000 Scots inside Hampden, but two first-half goals from midfielder Paul Scholes soon deflated the crowd. Scotland had chances, but failed to score.

A massive security operation failed to prevent some running battles on the streets of Glasgow. But like the match itself, they were a relatively low-key affair. Scotland now need an unlikely triumph at Wembley in the second leg if they are to qualify for the finals. (→ November 17)

England manager Kevin Keegan: he called his team's win a victory for "collective spirit".

More than 200 dead in EgyptAir disaster

US coastguards today called off the search for survivors from EgyptAir Flight 990, which crashed into the Atlantic early yesterday morning with 217 people on board. The Boeing 767 had stopped off at New York en route from Los Angeles to Cairo. It took off again at 1.20 a.m. Thirty minutes later it suddenly went into free fall, dropping 14,000 ft in 36 seconds before disappearing from air-traffic control radar screens.

The aircraft crashed off Nantucket, near where John F. Kennedy Jr's aircraft came down last July. Coastguards hope to find the "black box" flight recorders which may help explain the disaster. (→ November 16)

WEMBLEY, WEDNESDAY 17

Scotland win 1-0 but England go through

After England's 2-0 win over Scotland on Saturday, Scottish captain Colin Hendry said it would take "a ridiculously impressive performance" in the second leg of the play-off if the Scots were to reach the European Championship finals. "Ridiculously impressive" is precisely what Scotland were this evening, but it was still not enough to secure qualification.

The Scots ran England ragged, looking by far the more confident, accomplished team. A goal by Don Hutchinson gave them the lead after 39 minutes, but England clung on to reach the finals, 2-1 up on aggregate. For Scottish fans, however, their first victory over England in 14 years was cause enough for celebration.

London, Saturday 6. Former Spice Girl Geri Halliwell is hoping to top the singles chart with *Lift Me Up*, exploiting the media frenzy excited by her newly announced romance with Chris Evans. Cynical observers suggest that the relationship is a publicity stunt that will not last.

LAS VEGAS, SUNDAY 14

Britain's champion of the century

British boxer Lennox Lewis on top of the world after defeating Evander Holyfield.

In the early hours of this morning, Lennox Lewis became the first British boxer in the 20th century to be generally recognized as the heavyweight champion of the world. Already holder of the World Boxing Council (WBC) title, Lewis defeated Evander Holyfield, the World Boxing Association (WBA) and International Boxing Federation (IBF) champion, on points at Las Vegas's Thomas and Mack's Center.

Ironically, Lewis's dominance was less clear-cut than in his previous bout with Holyfield in March, when he was denied victory by an apparently bizarre decision of the ringside judges. Lewis had to resist a powerful onslaught from his American opponent in the middle rounds of the bout, but this time the judges' opinion went unanimously in his favour.

As Lewis's celebrations got under way, the IBF announced that it was refusing to recognize him as champion because of his team's failure to hand over money that should have been lodged with the organization before the fight. However, the news had little impact on the boxing world, which mostly seemed ready to accept Lewis as undisputed world champion. Lewis himself had no doubts: "I told you I was the best heavyweight in the world," he said, "and tonight I proved it."

SYDNEY AND CARDIFF, SATURDAY 6

Australians keep the Queen and win the Cup

Monarchists celebrated today after 55 per cent of Australians rejected a proposal for the country to become a republic. Instead, the Queen will remain head of state. Many Australians who supported a republic in principle had objected to the proposed replacement for the Queen, a president elected by the Australian parliament.

Defeated Australian republicans found solace in the rugby World Cup final, contested today at Cardiff's Millennium Stadium. Australia beat France comfortably 35-12, and the Queen was there to present the trophy to the Wallabies' captain, John Eales – a player noted for his pro-republican views.

The Queen presents Australia's rugby captain, John Eales, with the World Cup.

Facts and figures

Sport

MOTOR RACING

FORMULA ONE DRIVERS' CHAMPIONSHIP

	Driver	Points		Driver	Points
1	Mika Hakkinen (Finland)	76	7	Rubens Barrichello (Brazil)	21
2	Eddie Irvine (UK)	74	8	Johnny Herbert (UK)	15
3	Heinz-Harald Frentzen (Germany)	54	9	Giancarlo Fisichella (Italy)	13
4	David Coulthard (UK)	48	10	Mika Salo (Finland)	10
5	Michael Schumacher (Germany)	44	11	Damon Hill (UK)	7
6	Ralf Schumacher (Germany)	35	11=	Jarno Trulli (Italy)	7

HORSE RACING

ENGLISH CLASSIC WINNERS

Vodafone Derby
Oath ridden by Kieren Fallon

Vodafone Oaks
Ramruma ridden by Kieren Fallon

Sagitta 1000 Guineas
Wince ridden by Kieren Fallon

Sagitta 2000 Guineas
Island Sands ridden by Frankie Dettori

Rothmans St Leger
Mutafaweq ridden by Richard Hills

LEADING NATIONAL HUNT RACE WINNERS

Grand National
Bobby Jo ridden by Paul Carberry

Cheltenham Gold Cup
See More Business ridden by Mick Fitzgerald

Smurfit Champion Hurdle
Istabraq ridden by Charlie Swan

GOLF

WINNERS OF MAJOR TOURNAMENTS

Major	Venue	Winner
British Open	Carnoustie	Paul Lawrie (Scotland)
US Open	Pinehurst	Payne Stewart (USA)
US Masters	Augusta National	Jose Maria Olazabal (Spain)
US PGA	Medinah Country Club	Tiger Woods (USA)

LEADING MONEY WINNERS OF 1999

USA

1	Tiger Woods (USA)	$5,616,585
2	David Duval (USA)	$3,641,906
3	Davis Love III (USA)	$2,405,328
4	Vijay Singh (Fiji)	$2,213,233
5	Payne Stewart (USA)	$2,077,950

Europe

1	Colin Montgomerie (Scot.)	£1,269,879
2	Sergio Garcia (Spain)	£858,937
3	Lee Westwood (England)	£835,767
4	Retief Goosen (S. Africa)	£731,688
5	Paul Lawrie (Scotland)	£622,869

Little-known Scottish golfer Paul Lawrie, aged 30, had a tremendous year that included victory at the British Open.

TENNIS

GRAND SLAM SINGLES WINNERS

Wimbledon
Pete Sampras (USA)
Lindsay Davenport (USA)

US Open
Andre Agassi (USA), Serena Williams (USA)

French Open
Andre Agassi (USA), Steffi Graf (Germany)

Australian Open
Yevgeny Kafelnikov (Russia)
Martina Hingis (Switzerland)

CRICKET

AUSTRALIA V ENGLAND TEST SERIES

Test	Venue	Result
1st Test	Brisbane	Drawn
2nd Test	Perth	Australia won by 7 wickets
3rd Test	Adelaide	Australia won by 205 runs
4th Test	Melbourne	England won by 12 runs
5th Test	Sydney	Australia won by 98 runs

Australia won the series 3-1.

ENGLAND V NEW ZEALAND TEST SERIES

Test	Venue	Result
1st Test	Edgbaston	England won by 7 wickets
2nd Test	Lord's	New Zealand won by 9 wickets
3rd Test	Old Trafford	Drawn
4th Test	Oval	New Zealand won by 83 runs

New Zealand won the series 2-1.

MAJOR COUNTY TROPHIES

County Championship
Champions — Surrey
Runners-up — Lancashire

Benson & Hedges Super Cup
Final — Gloucestershire beat Yorkshire

National League First Division
Champions — Lancashire
Runners-up — Worcestershire

National League Second Division
Champions — Sussex
Runners-up — Somerset

NatWest Trophy
Final — Gloucestershire beat Somerset

CRICKET WORLD CUP 1999

GROUP A

	P	W	L	NR	Pts	RR
South Africa	5	4	1	0	8	0.86
India	5	3	2	0	6	1.28
Zimbabwe	5	3	2	0	6	0.02
England	5	3	2	0	6	-0.33
Sri Lanka	5	2	3	0	4	-0.81
Kenya	5	0	5	0	0	-1.20

NR: No result RR: Net run rate

GROUP B

	P	W	L	NR	Pts	RR
Pakistan	5	4	1	0	8	0.51
Australia	5	3	2	0	6	0.73
New Zealand	5	3	2	0	6	0.58
West Indies	5	3	2	0	6	0.50
Bangladesh	5	2	3	0	4	-0.52
Scotland	5	0	5	0	0	-1.93

NR: No result RR: Net run rate

SUPER SIX

	P	W	L	NR	Pts	RR
Pakistan	5	3	2	0	6	0.65
Australia	5	3	2	0	6	0.36
South Africa	5	3	2	0	6	0.17
New Zealand	5	2	2	1	5	-0.52
Zimbabwe	5	2	2	1	5	-0.79
India	5	1	4	0	2	-0.15

NR: No result RR: Net run rate

SEMI-FINALS

Pakistan beat New Zealand by 9 wickets

Australia tied with South Africa (Australia went through to the final on run rate)

FINAL

Australia beat Pakistan by 8 wickets

SOCCER

FA CARLING PREMIERSHIP 1998–99

		P	W	D	L	F	A	Pts
1	Manchester United	38	22	13	3	80	37	79
2	Arsenal	38	22	12	4	59	17	78
3	Chelsea	38	20	15	3	57	30	75
4	Leeds	38	18	13	7	62	34	67
5	West Ham	38	16	9	13	46	53	57
6	Aston Villa	38	15	10	13	51	46	55
7	Liverpool	38	15	9	14	68	49	54
8	Derby County	38	13	13	12	40	45	52
9	Middlesbrough	38	12	15	11	48	54	51
10	Leicester City	38	12	13	13	40	46	49
11	Tottenham Hotspur	38	11	14	13	47	50	47
12	Sheffield Wednesday	38	13	7	18	41	42	46
13	Newcastle United	38	11	13	14	48	54	46
14	Everton	38	11	10	17	42	47	43
15	Coventry	38	11	9	18	39	51	42
16	Wimbledon	38	10	12	16	40	63	42
17	Southampton	38	11	8	19	37	64	41
18	Charlton	38	8	12	18	41	56	36
19	Blackburn	38	7	14	17	38	52	35
20	Nottingham Forest	38	7	9	22	35	69	30

Relegated: Charlton, Blackburn, Nottingham Forest.

NATIONWIDE LEAGUE

	DIVISION 1	DIVISION 2	DIVISION 3
Champions	Sunderland	Fulham	Brentford
Runners–up	Bradford	Walsall	Cambridge United
Also promoted	Watford	Manchester City	Cardiff
			Scunthorpe
Relegated	Bury	York	Scarborough
	Oxford United	Northampton	
	Bristol City	Lincoln City	
		Macclesfield Town	

BANK OF SCOTLAND SCOTTISH PREMIER LEAGUE 1998–99

		P	W	D	L	F	A	Pts
1	Rangers	36	23	8	5	78	31	77
2	Celtic	36	21	8	7	84	35	71
3	St Johnstone	36	15	12	9	39	38	57
4	Kilmarnock	36	14	14	8	47	29	56
5	Dundee	36	13	7	16	36	56	46
6	Hearts	36	11	9	16	44	50	42
7	Motherwell	36	10	11	15	35	54	41
8	Aberdeen	36	10	7	19	43	71	37
9	Dundee United	36	8	10	18	37	48	34
10	Dunfermline	36	4	16	16	28	59	28

Dunfermline relegated.

MAJOR CUP FINALS IN ENGLAND

FA Cup (sponsored by Axa)	Manchester United 2	Newcastle United 0
Worthington Cup	Tottenham Hotspur 1	Leicester City 0

MAJOR CUP FINALS IN SCOTLAND

Tennents Scottish Cup	Rangers 1	Celtic 0
Scottish League Cup	Rangers 2	St Johnstone 1

MAJOR EUROPEAN CUP FINALS

European Champions' Cup	Manchester United 2	Bayern Munich 1
UEFA Cup	Parma 3	Marseille 0
European Cup Winners' Cup	Lazio 2	Real Mallorca 1

SNOOKER

WINNERS OF MAJOR TOURNAMENTS IN 1998–99

Embassy World Professional Championship
Stephen Hendry (Scotland)

Benson & Hedges Masters
John Higgins (Scotland)

Grand Prix
John Higgins (Scotland)

British Open
Stephen Hendry (Scotland)

Snooker champion Stephen Hendry.

RUGBY

DOMESTIC COMPETITIONS

Competition	Winner	Competition	Winner
Silk Cut Challenge Cup	Leeds Rhinos	Allied Dunbar Premiership	Leicester
JJB Super League	St Helens	Tetley's Bitter Cup	Wasps

FIVE NATIONS CHAMPIONSHIP

	P	W	D	L	F	A	Pts
Scotland	4	3	0	1	120	79	6
England	4	3	0	1	103	78	6
Wales	4	2	0	2	109	126	4
Ireland	4	1	0	3	66	90	2
France	4	1	0	3	75	100	2

RUGBY WORLD CUP

POOL A	P	W	D	L	F	A	Pts
South Africa	3	3	0	0	132	35	9
Scotland	3	2	0	1	120	58	7
Uruguay	3	1	0	2	42	97	5
Spain	3	0	0	3	18	122	3

POOL B	P	W	D	L	F	A	Pts
New Zealand	3	3	0	0	176	28	9
England	3	2	0	1	184	47	7
Tonga	3	1	0	2	47	171	5
Italy	3	0	0	3	35	196	3

POOL C	P	W	D	L	F	A	Pts
France	3	3	0	0	108	52	9
Fiji	3	2	0	1	124	68	7
Canada	3	1	0	2	114	82	5
Namibia	3	0	0	3	42	186	3

POOL D	P	W	D	L	F	A	Pts
Wales	3	2	0	1	118	71	7
Samoa	3	2	0	1	97	72	7
Argentina	3	2	0	1	83	51	7
Japan	3	0	0	3	24	107	3

POOL E	P	W	D	L	F	A	Pts
Australia	3	3	0	0	135	31	9
Ireland	3	2	0	1	100	45	7
Romania	3	1	0	2	50	126	5
United States	3	0	0	3	52	135	3

PLAY-OFFS
England 45 Fiji 24
Scotland 35 Samoa 20
Argentina 28 Ireland 24

QUARTER FINALS
South Africa 44 England 21
France 47 Argentina 26
New Zealand 30 Scotland 18
Australia 24 Wales 9

SEMI-FINALS
Australia 27 South Africa 21
France 43 New Zealand 31

FINAL
Australia 35 France 12

Andy Ward of Ireland tackles Ben Tune of Australia during the Rugby World Cup. Australia went on to win the tournament.

Awards

NOBEL PRIZES

Literature
Günter Grass (Germany)

Peace
Médecins Sans Frontières (France)

Physiology or Medicine
Dr Günter Blobel (USA)

Chemistry
Professor Ahmed Zewail (USA)

Physics
Professor Gerardus 'T Hooft (Netherlands)
Professor Martinus Veltman (Netherlands)

Economic Sciences
Professor Robert A. Mundell (USA)

ACADEMY AWARDS ("OSCARS")

Best Picture
Shakespeare in Love

Best Director
Steven Spielberg for *Saving Private Ryan*

Best Actress
Gwyneth Paltrow for *Shakespeare in Love*

Best Actor
Roberto Benigni for *Life Is Beautiful*

Best Supporting Actress
Judi Dench for *Shakespeare in Love*

Best Supporting Actor
James Coburn for *Affliction*

Best Original Musical Score
Stephen Warbeck for *Shakespeare in Love*

Best Foreign-language Film
Life Is Beautiful (Italy)

Best Cinematography
Janusz Kaminski for *Saving Private Ryan*

Best Original Screenplay
Marc Norman and Tom Stoppard for *Shakespeare in Love*

Best Adapted Screenplay
Bill Condon for *Gods and Monsters*

Best Art Direction
Martin Childs and Jill Quertier for *Shakespeare in Love*

Best Original Song
"When You Believe" from *The Prince of Egypt* – music & lyrics by Stephen Schwartz

Best Sound
Saving Private Ryan

Best Costume
Shakespeare in Love

Best Film Editing
Saving Private Ryan

Honorary Oscar
Elia Kazan

CANNES INTERNATIONAL FILM FESTIVAL

Palme d'Or
Rosetta directed by Luc and Jean-Pierre Dardenne (Belgium)

Grand Jury Prize
L'Humanité directed by Bruno Dumont (France)

Best Director
Pedro Almodóvar for *Todo Sobre Mi Madre* (Spain)

Best Screenplay
Yuri Arabov and Marina Koreneva for *Moloch* (Russia)

Best Actor
Emmanuel Schotté for *L'Humanité* (France)

Best Actress (shared)
Séverine Caneele for *L'Humanité* (France) and Emilie Dequenne for *Rosetta* (Belgium)

Special Jury Prize
The Letter directed by Manoel de Oliveira (Portugal)

BAFTA AWARDS

FILM AWARDS

Academy Fellowship
Elizabeth Taylor

Best Film
Shakespeare in Love

Best Actress
Cate Blanchett for *Elizabeth*

Best Actor
Roberto Benigni for *Life Is Beautiful*

Best Supporting Actor
Geoffrey Rush for *Shakespeare in Love*

Best Supporting Actress
Judi Dench for *Shakespeare in Love*

Best Original Screenplay
Andrew Niccol for *The Truman Show*

Best Special Effects
Saving Private Ryan

Best Director (David Lean Award)
Peter Weir for *The Truman Show*

Outstanding British Contribution to Cinema (Michael Bolcon Award)
Michael Kuhn

Outstanding British Film (Alexander Korda Award)
Elizabeth

TELEVISION AWARDS

Best Single Drama
A Rather English Marriage

Best Drama Series
Cops

Best Drama Serial
Our Mutual Friend

Best Actress
Dame Thora Hird for *Waiting for the Telegram*

Best Actor
Tom Courtenay for *A Rather English Marriage*

Best Comedy Performance
Dermot Morgan for *Father Ted*

Best Comedy
Father Ted

Best Light Entertainment Performance
Michael Parkinson for *Parkinson*

Best Light Entertainment
Who Wants to Be a Millionaire?

Best Soap
EastEnders

BRIT AWARDS

Best British Male Solo Artist
Robbie Williams

Best British Female Solo Artist
Des'ree

Best British Group
Manic Street Preachers

Best Video by a British Artist
Robbie Williams, *Millennium*

Best Album by a British Artist
Manic Street Preachers, *This Is My Truth Tell Me Yours*

Best British Newcomer
Belle & Sebastian

Best British Dance Act
Fatboy Slim

Best British Single
Robbie Williams, *Angels*

Best International Male Solo Artist
Beck

Best International Female Solo Artist
Natalie Imbruglia

Best International Group
The Corrs

Best International Newcomer
Natalie Imbruglia

Best Soundtrack/Cast Recording
Titanic

Outstanding Contribution to British Music
Eurythmics

THE BOOKER PRIZE

Winner
J.M. Coetzee, *Disgrace*

Shortlist
Anita Desai, *Fasting, Feasting*
Michael Frayn, *Headlong*
Andrew O'Hagan, *Our Fathers*
Ahdaf Soueif, *The Map of Love*
Colm Tóibín, *The Blackwater Lightship*

Former Take That member Robbie Williams was one of the top winners at this year's Brit Awards.

OLIVIER THEATRE AWARDS

Best Actress in a Play
Eileen Atkins for *The Unexpected Man*

Best Actor in a Play
Kevin Spacey for *The Iceman Cometh*

Best Director
Howard Davies for *The Iceman Cometh*

Best New Musical
Kat and the Kings

Best Actress in a Musical
Sophie Thompson for *Into the Woods*

Best Actor in a Musical
The cast of *Kat and the Kings*

Outstanding Musical Production
The National Theatre for *Oklahoma!*

Best New Comedy
Cleo, Camping, Emmanuelle and Dick by Terry Johnson

Best New Opera Production
Welsh National Opera, *La Clemenza di Tito*

Outstanding Achievement in Opera
The orchestra of the Royal Opera House

Outstanding Achievement in Dance
William Forsythe and his company at Sadler's Wells

Politics and Finance

THE CABINET

(November 1999)

Prime Minister Tony Blair

Deputy Prime Minister and Transport, Environment, and Regions Secretary John Prescott

Chancellor of the Exchequer Gordon Brown

Foreign and Commonwealth Secretary Robin Cook

Lord Chancellor Lord Irvine of Lairg

Home Secretary Jack Straw

Education and Employment Secretary David Blunkett

President of the Council and Leader of the House of Commons Margaret Beckett

Minister for the Cabinet Office and Chancellor of the Duchy of Lancaster Mo Mowlam

Defence Secretary Geoff Hoon

Health Secretary Alan Milburn

Chief Whip Ann Taylor

Culture, Media, and Sport Secretary Chris Smith

Scottish Secretary John Reid

Northern Ireland Secretary Peter Mandelson

Welsh Secretary Paul Murphy

International Development Secretary Clare Short

Social Security Secretary Alistair Darling

Minister for Agriculture, Fisheries, and Food Nick Brown

Leader of the Lords and Minister for Women Baroness Jay of Paddington

Trade and Industry Secretary Stephen Byers

Chief Secretary to the Treasury Andrew Smith

SCOTTISH CABINET

First Minister Donald Dewar

Deputy First Minister and Minister for Justice Jim Wallace

Minister for Social Inclusion, Local Government, and Housing Wendy Alexander

Minister for Transport and the Environment Sarah Boyack

Minister for Health and Community Care Susan Deacon

Minister for Rural Affairs Ross Finnie

Minister for Children and Education Sam Galbraith

Lord Advocate Lord Hardie

Business Manager Tom McCabe

WELSH CABINET

First Minister Alun Michael

Minister for Agriculture and Rural Development Christine Gwyther

Finance Secretary Edwina Hart

Health and Social Services Secretary Jane Hutt

Environment and Local Government Secretary Peter Law

Economic Development Secretary Rhodri Morgan

Education and Children Secretary Rosemary Butler

Education and Training Secretary Tom Middlehurst

Business Secretary Andrew Davies

FINANCE

INTEREST RATES

The chart on the right shows the bank base rate from December 1998 to November 1999. The rate was set at 6.75 per cent in November 1998. It is set monthly by the monetary policy committee of the Bank of England.

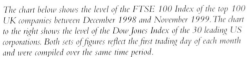

D J F M A M J J A S O N

SHARE PRICES

The chart below shows the level of the FTSE 100 Index of the top 100 UK companies between December 1998 and November 1999. The chart to the right shows the level of the Dow Jones Index of the 30 leading US corporations. Both sets of figures reflect the first trading day of each month and were compiled over the same time period.

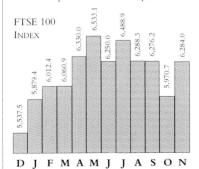

FTSE 100 INDEX

5,537.5 5,879.4 6,012.4 6,060.9 6,330.0 6,533.1 6,250.0 6,488.9 6,288.3 6,276.2 5,970.7 6,284.0

D J F M A M J J A S O N

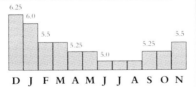

DOW JONES INDEX

9,089.0 9,184.3 9,345.7 9,324.8 9,832.5 10,596.3 10,886.1 11,066.4 10,677.3 10,937.9 10,336.9 10,648.5

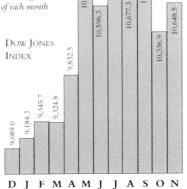

D J F M A M J J A S O N

Obituaries

George C. Scott, who won an Oscar for best actor for Patton, *died on September 22, 1999.*

Bart, Lionel, composer of musicals, born August 1, 1930, died April 3, 1999.

Bogarde, Sir Dirk, actor and novelist, born March 28, 1921, died May 8, 1999.

Casson, Sir Hugh, architect, born May 23, 1910, died August 15, 1999.

Clark, Alan, Tory politician, born April 13, 1928, died September 5, 1999.

Cockerell, Sir Christopher, inventor, born June 4, 1910, died June 1, 1999.

Dando, Jill, TV presenter, born November 9, 1961, died April 26, 1999.

Denning, Lord, judge, born January 23, 1899, died March 5, 1999.

DiMaggio, Joe, American baseball player, born November 25, 1914, died March 8, 1999.

Evans, Godfrey, Kent and England wicketkeeper, born August 18, 1920, died May 3, 1999.

Grade, Lord Lew, show business entrepreneur, born December 25, 1906, died December 13, 1998.

Hassan II, king of Morocco, born July 9, 1929, died July 23, 1999.

Heron, Patrick, artist, born January 30, 1920, died March 20, 1999.

Hume, Cardinal Basil, leader of the Catholic church in England and Wales, born March 2, 1923, died June 17, 1999.

Hussein, king of Jordan, born November 14, 1935, died February 7, 1999.

Kennedy, John F., Jr, publisher, born November 25, 1960, died July 16, 1999.

Kubrick, Stanley, film director, born July 26, 1928, died March 7, 1999.

Marshall, Malcolm, West Indian fast bowler, born April 18, 1958, died November 4, 1999.

Menuhin, Lord Yehudi, violinist, born April 22, 1916, died March 12, 1999.

Mitchison, Naomi, feminist writer, born November 1, 1897, died January 11, 1999.

Moore, Brian, Ulster-born novelist, born August 25, 1921, died January 10, 1999.

Morris, Johnny, TV presenter of *Animal Magic,* born June 20, 1916, died May 6, 1999.

Murdoch, Iris, novelist and philosopher, born July 15, 1919, died February 8, 1999.

Newley, Anthony, actor, singer, and composer, born September 24, 1931, died April 14, 1999.

Nimmo, Derek, comic actor on radio and TV, born September 19, 1930, died February 24, 1999.

Nyerere, Julius, former president of Tanzania, born April 13, 1922, died October 14, 1999.

Owen, Bill, actor who starred in *Last of the Summer Wine,* born March 14, 1914, died July 12, 1999.

Ramsey, Sir Alf, England football manager, born January 22, 1920, died April 28, 1999.

Reed, Oliver, actor, born February 13, 1938, died May 2, 1999.

Rollason, Helen, television sports broadcaster, born March 11, 1956, died August 8, 1999.

Scott, George C., American actor, born October 18, 1927, died September 22, 1999.

Soper, Lord Donald, Methodist preacher and social activist, born January 31, 1903, died December 22, 1998.

Springfield, Dusty, 1960s pop singer, born April 16, 1939, died March 2, 1999.

Stewart, Payne, American golfer, born January 30, 1957, died October 25, 1999.

Sutch, David E. "Screaming Lord", founder of the Official Monster Raving Loony Party, born November 12, 1940, died June 16, 1999.

Tormé, Mel, singer and songwriter, born September 13, 1925, died June 5, 1999.

Vaughan, Frankie, romantic singer, born February 3, 1928, died September 17, 1999.

Whitelaw, Viscount William, Tory politician, born June 28, 1918, died July 1, 1999.

Wise, Ernie, part of the comedy duo Morecambe and Wise, born November 27, 1925, died March 21, 1999.